Celebrate!®

WITH PARTY SPECTACULARS from A TO Z

EDITED BY EUGENE T.
AND MARILYNN C.
SULLIVAN

WILTON ENTERPRISES, INC., WOODRIDGE, ILLINOIS

OTHER WILTON BOOKS
The Wilton Way of Cake Decorating, Volume One
The Wilton Way of Cake Decorating, Volume Two
The Wilton Way of Cake Decorating, Volume Three
Discover the Fun of Cake Decorating
Beautiful Bridal Cakes the Wilton Way
The Wilton Book of Wedding Cakes
The Wilton Way to Decorate for Christmas
The Wilton Way of Making Gum Paste Flowers
Celebrate! Omnibus
Celebrate! II
Celebrate! III
Celebrate! IV
Celebrate! V
Celebrate! VI
Celebrate! Christmas
Celebrate! Wedding Cakes
The Complete Wilton Book of Candy

Celebrate!
WITH PARTY SPECTACULARS FROM A to Z

CO-EDITORS: Marilynn C. and Eugene T. Sullivan
PRODUCTION ASSISTANT: Ethel LaRoche
ART ASSISTANTS: Jim Artman, Ewald Weber
PHOTOGRAPHY: Tom Kasper
DECORATORS:
Wesley Kinsey
Debbie Kelly
Susan Matusiak
Amy Rohr

FIRST EDITION

Editorial mail should be addressed to:
Wilton Enterprises, Inc.
Book Division
2240 West 75th Street
Woodridge, Illinois 60517

Library of Congress Cataloging in Publication Data
Main entry under title:
Celebrate! with Party Spectaculars from A to Z
Includes index.
1. Cake decorating. I. Sullivan, Eugene T.
II. Sullivan, Marilynn.
TX771.C38 1983   641.8'653   83-21648
ISBN 0-912696-27-3

Celebrate! with Party Spectaculars from A to Z
is published by Wilton Enterprises, Inc.

When we asked decorators from all over the country what they would like to see in this new *Celebrate!*, they responded enthusiastically. So here is an exciting new book with over 150 *all new* cakes and treats—ones you asked for, and many more done in newly developed techniques we know you'll love. It's a star-studded collection from *Anniversary* cakes to a very *Zany* confection!

Everything in the book is shown close-up, in full color so you can see all the details. You'll enjoy brilliant cakes for teen-agers, some very handsome men's cakes, lots of very pretty cakes that are easy to decorate. Cakes for decorators who like a challenge, too. Just leaf through the pages and have the fun of discovering scores of decorated delights for yourself.

Many of you have asked for information on candy, too. We've included lots of luxurious, but easily done, new recipes. Some surprising new techniques for candy, too—never shown before.

For your convenience, we have also published a companion book, containing all the patterns you'll need for any project in this book.

As always, we would appreciate your comments. We consider them all carefully.

Happy decorating, and *Celebrate!*

VINCENT A. NACCARATO
President, Wilton Enterprises, Inc.

The Decorator's alphabet

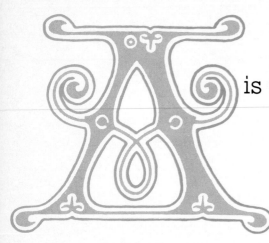 is for <u>Angel</u> cakes to serve at any season. <u>Anniversary</u> cakes, from the first to the twenty-fifth, and for <u>Amazing Animal</u> cakes.

Trim your Angel with a variety of decorating techniques to present it at its most beguiling.

Valentine Angel

See how poured fondant gives a smooth, glistening coating to this sweet angel—quickly, easily!

1. Bake a cake in the Cupid's Heart pan, chill and brush off loose crumbs. Attach to cake board, cut the same size and shape.

2. First put on a buttercream base. To accentuate the arm and hand, outline them with tube 2. Use tube 12 to build up arm and shoulder. Build up hand and fingers with tube 3. Smooth with a damp artist's brush. Ice top of heart and cupid, then smooth with a small, angled spatula. Set cake on rack over a cookie sheet.

3. Make a recipe of quick poured fondant and pour it over the iced area, using an artist's brush to keep fondant from puddling around fingers and forearm. Now pipe a tube 7 ball for nose with the cooled fondant.

4. Buttercream does all the rest of the decorating. Write message with tube 2 and thinned icing. Cover sides of heart with tube 16 stars, bringing them up over curved edge. Pipe curls for hair with tube 16. Pipe a ruffle around heart with tube 126, starting and stopping at arm. Finish heart with tube 2 beading. Use tube 115 to pipe fluffy feathers for wing, starting at bottom and covering

side of cake. Now add two tube 4 balls for eyes and a tube 2 smile. Dilute pink food color with a few drops of water and paint on round cheeks. Attach satin ribbon with fondant. Serve to twelve.

Merry Christmas Angel

This cheery greeting is decorated mainly in the traditional star technique in buttercream.

1. Prepare cake and build up shoulder, arm and fingers just as described for Valentine angel. Pipe holly leaves and freeze.

2. Cover heart surface with icing and smooth with a spatula. Write message with tube 2. Cover angel and sides of heart with tube 17 stars. Do hair with tube 16, eyes with tube 4, mouth with tube 2.

3. Pipe tube 126 feathers on wings, starting at base of cake and working up. Pipe a tube 126 ruffle around heart and edge with tube 2 beading. Attach holly and add tube 4 red berries. Serve to twelve.

Anniversary Angel

Smoothed buttercream covers angel and heart, with stars covering the ribbon drape.

1. Pipe drop flowers with tube 131, freeze or dry. Prepare cake and build up shoulder, arm and hand just as for Valentine angel. Ice heart smoothly. Ice angel, then smooth with a warm spatula. Write message with tube 2.

2. Pipe hair with tube 16 curls. Add tube 4 eyes and nose, tube 2 smile. Pipe feathers on wings with

tube 402, drape with tube 16.

3. Edge heart with a tube 125 ruffle, then pipe leaves with tube 67. Press on prepared drop flowers. Add more drop flowers and leaves to trim ribbon drape. As a final touch, pipe a little pink heart with tube 3. Serve to twelve.

An Angel cake for a baby

You'll find the rolled fondant that covers most of the area of this cake a dream to work on! Use a firm pound cake recipe.

1. Cover top of heart and angel area with a thin coating of buttercream. Smooth with a spatula. Make a recipe of rolled fondant. Break off about a quarter of the fondant, knead it, then roll out to about ⅛" thickness. Lay over the top of the heart, smooth with your hands, then trim off edges. Tint the remainder of the fondant flesh color, roll out and drape over the angel. Smooth the fondant with your hands, rounding it around the curves and emphasizing the indentations. Trim off neatly at base of cake and around hand and forearm.

2. Pipe message on heart with tube 2. Cover sides of heart with tube 16 stars. Do hair with tube 16, eyes and nose with tube 4, mouth with tube 2. Cover wing with tube 402 feathers. Pipe ruffle around heart with tube 125 and finish with tube 2 beading. Pipe pink hearts with tube 3. Attach ribbon with royal icing. Serve to twelve.

Married in May?

Adorn their cake with May's flower, lily of the valley. Crown it with five candles for their fifth anniversary. The time-saving secret of this lovely cake is the trim of dainty fabric flowers.

1. Bake, fill and ice the tiers. Base tier is a two-layer 10" x 4" round. Insert a circle of ¼" round dowel rods, clipped level with top of tier, to support tiers above. Three upper tiers are single-layer, baked in Round mini-tier pans.

2. To form the heart on side of base tier, spread buttercream thickly on wax paper. Cover with wax paper and roll gently to ⅛" thickness. Place this "sandwich" over a 10" cake-side former and freeze. Peel off top wax paper and cut into heart shape with a sharp knife and *Celebrate!* pattern. Leave heart attached to bottom wax paper. Return to freezer, still on former.

3. Decorate tiers separately. Mark pattern for heart in center of side of base tier. Run tube 1D around bottom, tube 2B around edge of top. Edge bottom of cake with a tube 5 border, add loops, dots and beading with tube 2. Remove heart from freezer and do lettering with tube 1. Brush heart area marked on cake with water. Carefully peel wax paper off heart and place on cake. Edge with tube 2 beading.

On bottom mini-tier, edge base and top with tube 48. Add tube 2 strings, dots and beading. On middle mini-tier, divide top edge into twelfths. Pipe radiating lines of tube 47 from center of tier top to marked edge, then down side to base. Pipe a tube 4 bulb border at base, then add tube 2 beading and scallops at top.

the fifth . . . and the first . . . happy year!

On top tier, edge base and top with tube 47 and finish with tube 2.

4. Assemble tiers with legs. Lay a circle of clear plastic on middle mini-tier. Insert four Flower spikes on base tier, adjacent to legs. Fill with flower sprays, then arrange more sprays on plastic circle. Insert candles in holders on top tier. Serve Mini-tiers to twelve, base tier to 14 guests.

Quick & Pretty
Two happy people . . .
celebrate their first anniversary.

To start their portraits, bake two single-layer cakes in the Bell pan set and set on cake boards cut the same size and shape. Bake a single cupcake, too.

1. Mark features on cakes with a toothpick, attempting to reproduce hair-do's and favorite clothing. Build up cheeks and chins with icing. For her cake, outline chin and neckline with tube 2, then fill in with tube 16 stars. Do hair with same tube. Pipe white areas of eyes with tube 10, flatten slightly, then add blue with tube 7. Pipe a

tube 4 smile. Do necklace with tube 16 stars and add a tube 5 heart pendant.

2. For his cake, trim off a little on each side to indicate shoulder. Use the same tubes as for her cake. As a final touch, pattern his necktie with tube 3 dots. Ice the cupcake, border with tube 14, then letter with tube 1. Add a single candle. Each portrait cake will serve six guests.

A lavish centerpiece for their 25th Anniversary

Make the celebration cake as important and beautiful as the occasion! This creation with its lofty stairway and flowery trim will set the tone of the party.

Assemble your accessories first. You will need:

- 16″ plate and four legs from the Tall tier set
- Two 12″ round separator plates
- Four Corinthian pillars
- Filigree stairway and bridge
- Lazy daisy server
- Frolicking cherub figure
- Numeral candy molds
- Heart ornament base
- Fabric flowers and silver leaves

Make trims ahead. Pipe many tube 225 drop flowers in royal icing. Mold "25" in Candy Melts™ confectionery coating. Trim with drop flowers and silver leaves. Turn bottom of Heart base upside down to form a bowl. Wedge a block of styrofoam into it and arrange flowers and leaves for top ornament. Do the same with plate of ornament base for a within-pillars ornament.

Prepare the cakes. Use a firm pound cake recipe. Satellite cake is 10″ round layer plus a 10″ top bevel layer. Base tier of main cake is a two-layer 14″ x 4″ round. Upper tier is a 10″ round layer plus a 10″ top bevel. Fill and ice the tiers with buttercream, then cover with rolled fondant.

Decorate satellite cake Divide cake side in twelfths and mark 2″ above base. Repeat markings at top edge of bevel. Set on lazy daisy server.

1. For base border, pipe a tube 10 line of icing around bottom. Cover with drop flowers. Drop tube 2 strings from mark to mark on cake side. Repeat for triple strings, then finish with dots.

2. On bevel surface, pipe zigzag tube 16 garlands from mark to mark. Cover with drop flowers.

Decorate main cake Assemble tiers on stand with pillars and plates. Divide bottom tier in twelfths and mark 1½″ above base. Repeat markings 1″ above first. On top tier, using pillars as guides, divide in twelfths and mark 1″ up from base. Mark again at top of bevel.

1. On bottom tier, pipe a tube 18 shell border at base. Pipe zigzag tube 16 garlands from mark to

mark. Cover with drop flowers. Drop tube 2 strings from marks, then repeat for triple strings. Add dots. Attach trios of drop flowers at points of strings with icing. Edge separator plate with tube 16 shells.

2. On top tier, pipe a tube 16 shell border at base. Pipe zigzag garlands from marks with the same tube. Press in drop flowers. Drop triple strings on bevel, then trim with drop flowers.

Add final touches of stairway and assembly.

1. For stairway carpet, use *Celebrate!* pattern to cut from rolled fondant. Cut top riser and tread separately. Smooth carpet over stair, trimming as necessary, and allow to dry. Remove carpet from top stair.

2. Assemble on the party table. Place main cake in position. Center within-pillars ornament. Ask a friend to shift satellite cake as you hold stairway above cakes. Press top of stairway into top tier, letting bottom rest on satellite cake. Place top stair carpet on stair.

Set bridge with bouquet on top tier. Support "25" on mounds of icing, leaning against bridge. Wire little nosegays of fabric flowers to stairway railings, then add the cherub figure. A marvelous centerpiece for an anniversary celebration! Cut into wedding-cake sized pieces. Main cake serves 140 guests. Present the satellite cake to the anniversary couple. It will serve 48.

Note: *with changes of color and ornament, this lovely cake would be suitable for a wedding reception.*

Amazing Animal cakes make everyone laugh!

Use your shaped pans and a little ingenuity to create a sensation! You don't need a holiday to serve one of these cheerful pets. Surprise the family, delight a child when he comes home from school—or ask the neighbors in for dessert.

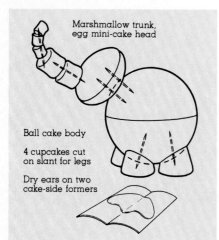

Marshmallow trunk, egg mini-cake head

Ball cake body

4 cupcakes cut on slant for legs

Dry ears on two cake-side formers

Eliza Elephant

Just as cute and cuddly as she can be! To make this peach-colored pet, you'll need four cupcakes, a 6" Ball cake, two egg Mini-cakes put together, marshmallows for trunk and marzipan for ears. Use a firm pound cake recipe for all cakes.

1. Tint marzipan, roll out to about ⅛" thickness and cut Eliza's ears, using Celebrate! pattern. Dry on two Cake-side formers.

2. Assemble the cake on a serving tray as diagram shows. Use icing and toothpicks to secure head and trunk. Pipe tube 16 stars all over, then pipe tube 4 eyes and mouth. Perky tail is a curve with tube 16.

3. Attach ears on mounds of icing, resting against body. For a flirtatious touch, add drop flowers and a ribbon bow.

Carlo Koala

Bright-eyed, inquisitive and intent on his diet of eucalyptus leaves! Carlo's body is carved from a loaf cake, his head is a small Wonder mold, his legs are figure piped and he's entirely friendly.

1. Bake cakes from a firm pound cake recipe. Allow Wonder mold cake to mound during baking. Chill, then assemble with toothpicks and carve body as diagram shows. Set on serving tray.

2. Pipe tree branch with long curved tube 16 lines. Pipe legs with tube 2A, starting with heavy pressure. Four-fingered "hands" are piped with tube 3. Crescent-shaped ears are done with tube 12.

3. Pipe nose and eyes with tube 10, then flatten with a damp fingertip. Cover entire body with tube 16 stars. Pull out fluffy fur on ears with same tube and pipe a tube 4 smile. Finish with tube 69 leaves.

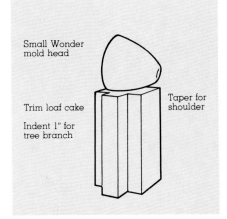

Theodore Bear

This is the pet that wins every popularity contest! Dress him up for a party with a ruffled collar and bow. Teddy's body is an 8" round layer plus a Wonder mold cake, head a 6" ball cake. Cupcakes make his nose and legs.

1. Construct body and legs on serving tray. Ice paws smoothly, then cover legs and body with tube 18 stars. Pipe a tube 127D ruffle at top of body.

2. Attach head on mound of icing with toothpicks. Add cupcake nose, flatten and shape marshmallows and attach for ears. Ice end of nose and ears smoothly. Pipe tube 12 eyes and flatten, tube 7 smile. Now cover with tube 18 stars. Give Ted a red ribbon bow.

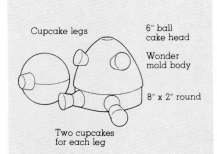

B is for Beautiful Birthday cakes!
Trim them with bright Balloons,
Blossoms or clever Borders—
they're the Best cakes of all!

A Balloon centerpiece

1. Figure pipe the clown first in figure piping icing stiffened with extra sugar (page 84). Pipe a tube 5 oval for head separately on wax paper and dry. Pipe tube 10 shell-shaped feet on wax paper, then use tube 1A for pear-shaped body. Add tube 5 arms, starting with light pressure, increasing as you go down. Pipe mitten-shape hands with tube 1. Do ruffles at waist and neck with tube 101, at wrists with tube 101s. Attach head and pipe features with tube 1. Give the clown a tube 4B pointed hat and tube 1s spiky hair. Dry.

2. For his balloons, stick stiff wire into ball-shaped cherry candies. Thin the icing and dip each candy three times, drying between dips. Insert wires into hand.

3. The rest of the decorating is quick and easy. Bake, fill and ice a two-layer 8" round cake. Also bake a dozen or more cupcakes. Divide cake into sixths and mark near base. Extending to each mark, pipe three tube 1 strings. Top with tube 12 balloons. Use a 6" cake circle to lightly mark a guide line for lettering, then pipe with tube 2. Finish the cake with tube 5 bulb borders and set clown on top.

4. Ice cupcakes with tube 4B swirls and insert candles. Center a large tray with the birthday cake and surround with cupcakes. Serve the cupcakes at the party—save the cake to serve to ten at a family celebration.

Hot air Balloon

1. Paint the top plate of a heart ornament base with thinned royal icing. Glue on four stud plates, as close together as possible. Paint a 4" square of corrugated cardboard and glue on four corresponding stud plates. With 5" clear pillars, you have the support for the balloon.

2. Bake a two-layer cake in 5" Mini-tier pans and a 6" ball cake. Use a firm pound cake recipe. Chill the cakes, then fill them.

Taper 5" cake to 4½" at base. Ice with buttercream and rough up with a damp sponge. Insert dowel rods, clipped level with top of cake, to support cake above.

Ice ball cake thinly, then divide in half horizontally, in eighths vertically with a taut string. Assemble with prepared pillars. Fill in areas with tube 16 stars.

3. The tailored trim is rolled marzipan. Use miniature cutters to cut out 24 diamonds, 16 hearts and 16 half-circles. Press shapes into icing. Attach gold cord to connect balloon with basket, securing with toothpicks. Add tube 3 balls. Banner is a ribbon glued to a toothpick, lettered with tube 1 and supported by marzipan circles. Arrange the soldier band passengers. Serve the balloon to twelve, basket to four guests.

Birthday cakes for the under-six set . . . each with a built-in bonus gift

Build a special treat right into the birthday cake—watch the little faces beam! Each of these pretty cakes is easy and fast to decorate, too.

Quick & Pretty

A pink candy teddy . . .

is a bonus for the birthday child who receives this cake, topped with blocks that spell out his name and age.

1. Mold the teddy bear in a two-piece stand-up mold in Candy Melts™ confectionery coating. Use the color contrast method on page 34. Trim seams with a small sharp knife. Smooth with a damp "Handi Wipe" and tie a ribbon round his neck. Pipe tube 225 and 129 drop flowers in royal icing.

2. Bake and chill a single-layer 9" x 13" sheet cake. Trim about 2½" off one short side and cut into four 2" cubes. Ice sheet cake. Hold each cube on fork to ice.

3. Divide longer sides of sheet cake in sevenths, shorter sides into fifths and mark midway on sides. Make corresponding marks on cake top, 1" in from edge. Run a tube 5 line around base of cake, then drop tube 104 swags from mark to mark. Pipe swags on cake top.

4. Holding cake cube on fork, pipe letters and numbers wtih tube 3, shell borders with tube 13. Arrange cubes on sheet cake, then add drop flower trim. Insert candles and pose Teddy! Serve cubes to four, sheet cake to nine guests.

Quick & Pretty

Lollipops for all . . .

are part of the trim of this impressive little tier cake. Mold the lollipops from Candy Melts™, then attach made-ahead drop flowers with dots of melted coating. Pipe tube 65 leaves.

1. Use the Mini-tier set to bake, ice and assemble the tiers. Pipe tube 190 drop flowers in royal icing and set aside to dry.

2. Pipe message with tube 2, shell borders at base of all tiers with tube 16. For top borders, attach flowers with dots of icing, then fill in with tube 67 leaves. Insert candles and lollipops and serve to twelve.

Quick & Pretty

A dainty figurine . . .

crowns the birthday cake and will be a treasured souvenir for the birthday child. To give a satin covering to the cake, use quick poured fondant. The fast, sweetly tailored trim is marzipan.

1. Bake a cake in the Wonder mold, ice smoothly with buttercream, then cover with quick poured fondant. Attach to foil-covered cake board.

2. Tint marzipan in dainty pastels and roll out. Using truffle and miniature cutters, cut out designs. Flower shapes are cut with the violet cutter from the Flower garden set, centers with tube 6. Attach designs in neat, tailored fashion with dots of buttercream. Insert candles in Push-in holders and trim with tiny marzipan hearts. For bottom border, form a cylinder of marzipan about 7" long, 1" thick. Roll with both hands to a long thin rope. Cut rope in two, if necessary, to continue rolling. "Braid" two ropes together, then wrap around cake. Set figurine on cake top and serve to twelve guests.

15

16

Quick & Pretty
Stuffed animal pets

Here are ingenious ways to use your shaped pans—and create charming birthday cakes for toddlers (teen-age girls, too!).

A calico cat

1. For her head, bake and fill two layers in the smallest Heart mini-tier pan. Trim off point of heart. Body is a one-layer oval cake. Carve out a curve from the oval cake, using heart pan as pattern, and fit the two cakes together on a serving tray. Use tube 12 to figure pipe paws and curving tail. Figure pipe pointed ears with tube 10.

2. Cover entire cat with tube 16 stars. Build up nose, mouth and eyes with tube 5. The rosebuds are tube 13 rosettes trimmed with tube 65 leaves. Dip pieces of spaghetti in thinned icing and push in for whiskers. Serves eight.

A polka dot dog

1. Start surprisingly with a cake baked in the Truck pan. Make a mark 2" up from the rear of the truck and cut off in a straight line. Cut this piece in two and attach on both sides of the front of the truck, long cut sides against cake. Here's a dog with floppy ears.

2. Use tube 12 to figure pipe two mounds for paws and build up front legs, tail, cheeks and chin. Use the same tube for eyes, nose and mouth. Outline areas with tube 3, then fill in with tube 16 stars. Add contrasting polka dots with the same tube. Add a bow and candles. Serves twelve.

Jump for Joy!

1. Prepare trims. Pipe royal icing drop flowers with tubes 129 and 131 and dry. Attach some to toothpicks with dots of icing and add tube 65s leaves. Tint Roll-out cookie dough and cut clowns with the boy Christmas cutter. Cut 1" circles from untinted dough and place on cookies for faces. Cut holes near tops of heads with a round tube. Bake. When cool,

dress up the clowns with small tubes and royal icing.

2. Bake, fill and ice a 10" round cake and a single-layer 6" round. Set each on a cardboard cake board. Bake a half-ball in the Ball pan. Assemble with 7½" Clear twist legs and a 6" clear plate. Push the legs through the 6" cake down to its cake board. Mark four curved arches on ball cake. Divide 10" cake in eighths, mark midway on side and drop strings from mark to mark to define curves.

3. On 10" cake, pull up columns on sides with tube 19. Fill in from curves to base with tube 16 stars. Pipe a tube 16 zigzag border on cake top. Pipe tube 19 zigzags to cover side of 6" cake. Cover half-ball with tube 16 stars in contrasting colors. Insert a toothpick in top and pipe tube 20 upright shells.

4. Pull nylon thread through holes in clowns' heads and tape ends to underside of plate. Plant flowers, trim with tube 65 leaves and insert candles in holders. Serves 23.

Make a teen very happy on her Birthday

There she is!

For that important 15th or 16th birthday, bake her a cake that's a replica of her pretty self, dressed in ruffles and ribbons, holding a dainty bouquet. Pipe the drop flowers in advance with tube 225.

1. Prepare the cakes. The stage is a single-layer 12″ round cake. Ice in buttercream, then inset a 6″ circle of dowel rods, clipped off level with the cake top. Bake a Wonder mold cake, set on cardboard cake circle and place on the 12″ cake. To elongate the waistline, ice a marshamallow to the top of the Wonder mold and add icing to smooth it into the shape of the cake. Insert Little girl doll pick. Divide base of skirt into eighths and mark curving lines up to waist to guide ruffles.

2. Cover skirt with tube 16 stars working from bottom up and stopping just short of guidelines. Starting at center front waistline, pipe the ruffles. For a graduated effect, start with tube 102 and light pressure. Increase pressure as you approach mid-point of the skirt, then change to tube 104. Again, start with light pressure and increase it as you curve around the hemline.

2. Cover bodice with tube 13 stars. Wire doll's hands. Pipe a mound of icing on hands and press in drop flowers. Finish the dress with a tube 104 ruffle at neckline.

3. On 12″ cake, pipe a shell-motion base border with tube 70. Use the same tube to pipe a ruffled top border. Insert candles in holders to spotlight the birthday girl! 12″ cake serves ten, Wonder mold serves twelve guests.

Her favorite food . . .

and that of every teenager! This treat is made of Candy Melts™ confectionery coating artfully tinted and shaped. It's really fun to do! Review the melting procedure for coating, page 42, and the method for cut-out trims, page 47.

1. *Crust* is molded in a 10″ round pan. To get the golden brown color, combine one pound of white wafers, six ounces of light chocolate and two ounces of yellow. After melted coating is poured in the pan, place on floor of freezer about five minutes or less to harden. Turn out of pan on wax paper, then pour a little melted coating around edges to round them off.

2. Use the cut-out method for the toppings. Add Candy colors to tint about ¼ pound of each color.

For olives, cut centers with small end of tube 2A, outside with wide end of same tube. *Onions* are cut in concentric circles with the four smallest cutters from the round cutter set. *Peppers* are ¼″ strips, *mushrooms* and *pepperoni* are cut freehand.

3. Set the pizza on a serving tray, then pour over it melted red coating for sauce. Scatter all the toppings over it. To add cheese, put melted coating in a paper cone, cut the tip and casually criss-cross the pizza. Surround with birthday candles. Bravo!

Fantastically garish, a stand-up juke box

Here it is, with all its wonderously pulsating lights and push-button selectors. What a way to say happy birthday to a teen! Read on to see how to build it.

1. Bake two cakes in the Juke box pan. Use a firm pound cake batter. For each cake you will need 6½ cups of pound cake mix batter (average box yields 3½ cups). Bake about 40 minutes. Chill the cakes, then ice flat surface of one, and place the other cake on it, back to back. Trim the base to flatten it and insert a few toothpicks for security. To decorate the front, let the juke box lie flat.

2. For decorating, use either Buttercream or Figure piping icing (reduce confectioners' sugar by one cup). Ice the red and blue center areas smoothly. Pipe message on blue area with tube 1. Pipe grille over red speaker area freehand with the same tube. Pipe the white ribbon with tube 1D and score with a knife.

Do the pink and purple "bubble tubes" with tube 403, following design on cake. Change to tube 402 for the orange, blue and green tubes.

3. Fill in the front of the juke box with tube 16 stars. Add the gold bars on the sides with tube 2A. Outline message area with tube 5. Use tube 12 to trim the red grill area and do triple bars on the top.

4. Now stand the juke box up on a serving tray. Fill in all remaining areas with tube 16 stars. Add candles. It's Play Time! Serve to 24.

Quick & Pretty

A zigzag cake

Just three tubes and icing in bright primary colors create a striking cake for his birthday.

1. Bake a two-layer 10″ x 4″ round cake. Fill and ice. Divide in twelfths and mark on side of cake 1″ up from base.

2. Pipe tube 8 bulb borders at bottom and top of cake. Pipe message with tube 1. Use tube 48 to pipe an inverted "V", from mark to mark, forming a zigzag border. Repeat twice more above first zigzag, changing color of icing. Use tube 48 again to pipe rosettes on cake top. Insert tapers in centers of rosettes. Serve to 14.

Dirt rider!

Thrill him with this stunning dirt bike! It's done in dimensional Color Flow, following *Celebrate!* patterns and rides across a sheet cake.

1. Do the bike in five pieces. Pipe curved frame with tube 6, then outline rest with tube 2. Fill in with thinned icing of a slightly heavier than usual texture, so areas round up. Dry thoroughly.

2. Bake and fill a two-layer 9" x 13" cake. Ice sides. Spread a smooth area of brown icing across center of cake. Let crust, then spread sky blue above brown, yellow below, in sweeping curves. Divide long sides of cake in eighths, short sides in fifths, and mark 1" up from base. Pipe curved "C's" with tube 18 from mark to mark. Pipe top border with tube 14 shells. Do birthday message on "sun" with tube 1.

3. Assemble bike on cake, supporting pieces on tube 4 over-piped lines for dimension. First support wheels on three lines. Pipe tube 1 dots on outer edges of wheels. Add main part of bike on five lines, then fender on four lines. Last attach fork on single lines where it touches wheel and fender. Pipe yellow stripe with tube 44, sand on wheels with tube 000. Attach sun on mound of icing. Surround cake with candles in Push-in holders. Serve to 24 cheering guests.

16 . . . now he can drive!

Give him his heart's desire—a pickup truck. Build this sweet model as the diagram shows. You will need a 12" x 18" sheet cake for

the lower part of the truck and a loaf cake for the cab. Cookies make the trim. Wheels are cut with 3″ round cutters, hub caps with 1½″ cutters, head lights with 1″ cutters. The two bumpers are ¾″ x 6″ cookie strips. Patterns for cookie windows are in *Celebrate! Pattern Book*. Use the Roll-out cookie recipe on page 85 or your own.

1. Bake cookies, cool and paint with thinned royal icing. Pipe messages on windows with tube 1. Cover an 8″ x 20″ cake board with foil. Ice a 4″ x 13″ block of 1″

styrofoam for support. Ice to cake board. Cut sheet cake in two, fill and stack. Trim to 16″ length. Place on 6″ x 16″ cardboard cake board. Add cab cake, then ice assembled cakes smoothly.

2. Pipe radiator grill with tube 789 and score with a knife. Attach bumpers, headlights and windows. Mark position of wheels on cake sides. Outline windows and door with tube 2. Pipe orange stripes and handle with tube 6 and outline truck bed with the same tube. Over-pipe for depth.

3. Put it all together with icing. Attach support to cake board, truck to support. Add cookie wheels. Fill the pickup bed with candles. Just what he wanted! Serves 30 guests.

Trim loaf cake for cab

Cut 12″ x 18″ cake in two.
Fill, stack and trim to 16″
Cardboard cake board
Styrofoam support   20″ x 8″ foil-covered board

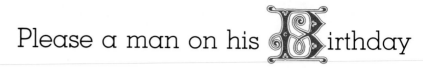

Make mine chocolate! Watch your man's eyes light up when you present him with one of these extravaganzas! Trim his cake with marzipan, lattice, full-blown roses or precise piping—but make it chocolate!

A marzipan plaque . . .

holds the message, framed with golden marzipan roses.

1. Make a recipe of marzipan, roll out about one-fourth of it and cut the plaque. Use your 9″ x 7″ oval pan as pattern. Tint another fourth of the marzipan and model the roses. Page 69 shows you how. Allow plaque and roses to set up overnight, then brush them with Corn syrup glaze.

2. Bake and fill a two-layer 9″ x 13″ cake. Ice with chocolate buttercream, then place plaque in center of cake top.

3. Decorating's fast and easy. Mark a curve from corner to corner on each side of cake. Outline curves with tube 16 stars, then fill in with stars down to base of cake. Use tube 16 again to pipe rosette top border. Pipe message with tube 1, then frame the plaque with tube 14 shells. Arrange roses on mounds of icing, then add tube 70 buttercream leaves. Serve to 24.

Chocolate leaves . . .

circle this elegant confection!

1. Pick about two dozen leaves from your garden, wash and gently

pat dry. (Rose leaves are ideal.) Cover a cookie sheet with wax paper. Melt about one-fourth pound of confectionary coating and cover undersides of leaves with an artist's brush. Lay coated leaves on cookie sheet and refrigerate about ten minutes until coating hardens. Peel off leaves, starting with stem. Refrigerate.

2. Bake a two-layer 10″ round cake. Fill and ice with chocolate buttercream. Cover cake with chocolate poured fondant.

3. Pipe message with tube 1 and thinned royal icing. Circle the cake top with triple scallops done at one time with quick tube 89. Now pipe a thick line of icing around base of cake and arrange

with a handsome chocolate cake

leaves. Insert candle. Serves 14.

Chocolate lattice . . .

enlivens a cake crowned with his age in candy numbers.

1. Mold numbers in Numeral mold with Candy Melts™ confectionary coating. Trim with tube 1. Pipe a few royal icing drop flowers with tube 190 and 225.

2. Bake a 10" square cake. Chill, cut in half, fill and stack to make a 10" x 5" two-layer cake. Ice in chocolate buttercream. Cut an oval pattern, 4" wide, 7" long and mark on cake top. Pipe a tube 1 message within oval. Mark sides for garlands, 1½" up from base.

3. Pipe a tube 16 base shell border. Drop string guidelines from mark to mark and cover with tube 16 zigzag garlands. Now pipe tube 1 lattice and triple strings. Frame lattice with tube 2 strings. Add dots. Pipe tube 1 lattice on cake top, edge with tube 14 shells. Place numbers, supporting on mounds of icing and toothpicks. Add taper. Trim with drop flowers and tube 65 leaves. Serve to ten.

Quick & Pretty

Chocolate and mocha!

Trim a mocha buttercream cake with chocolate—a winning combination! Pipe tube 124 roses in advance, then the decorating is very fast. The hexagon shape almost measures itself.

1. Bake and fill a two-layer 12" hexagon cake. Ice with mocha buttercream. Use chocolate buttercream for all decorating.

2. Pull up tube 19 "columns" at each corner of cake and top with fleurs-de-lis. Pipe shells at base with same tube. Drape tube 13 strings, add stars. Frame base border with zigzags with same tube. Pipe a tube 2 message on cake top, then add a tube 17 top shell border. Secure roses and trim with tube 70 leaves. Light the candles! Serve to 20 guests.

Make her **B**irthday cake frilly and feminine

Ladies of every age love flowers and flounces and dainty tints—so trim one of these sweet cakes for her birthday. Each cake has a time-saving decorating hint.

A garland of flowers

If you're one of those far-sighted decorators who save extra flowers from every decorating job, you'll put this lavish cake together in a hurry, just as we did. We selected about 30 roses, 30 sweet peas and ten daisies from our stock, all piped with tube 104, then added lots of drop flowers. All the flowers were made of royal icing. (They keep indefinitely.)

1. Bake a two-layer 10″ and a single-layer 6″ round cake. Ice both cakes with buttercream, then cover with Quick poured fondant. Assemble on serving tray.

2. At base of lower tier, pipe a series of tube 20 "C" curves to form border. Trim with curves of drop flowers and tube 65 leaves. Pipe a tube 16 shell border around base of upper tier. Write birthday message with tube 1.

3. Arrange the made-ahead flowers in a garland, tilting on mounds of icing. Add tube 67 leaves. Make six fluffy ribbon bows, wire to toothpicks and insert in cake. Finish with a curve of

candles. Serve this flowery treat to 17 guests.

Heart-shaped greetings

Mold rosy hearts from Candy Melts™ confectionery coating, add dainty flowers and the decorating's almost done!

1. Mold the hearts in Large and Small lollipop molds (close stick opening with foil) and Small heart molds. Write message on larger hearts with tube 1. (A mixture of royal icing and piping gel is easiest to use.) Pipe royal icing flowers with tube 35.

2. Bake, fill and ice a two-layer 9″ heart cake. Divide each side of

heart into fourths and mark midway on sides. Pipe a tube 16 shell border at base. Drop string guidelines for curves, then pipe garlands with tube 69 for a double ruffled effect. Use the same tube for a shell-motion top border.

3. Arrange candy hearts on cake top, edge with tube 3 beading and trim with drop flowers. Add tube 65 leaves. Insert birthday candles in a curve. Serve this sentimental treat to 12 guests.

A flowery sheet cake

Dress up an easy-to-serve sheet cake with curving flounces and her favorite wild roses.

1. Bake, fill and ice a two-layer 9" x 13" sheet cake. Mark curves for cake-top ruffles the easy way with 4" and 2½" round cutters. Divide long sides of cake into fifths, short sides into thirds and mark midway on sides. Drop string guidelines from mark to mark.

2. Pipe tube 16 shell borders at bottom and top edge. Write cake-top message with tube 2. Do fluted ruffles on sides with tube 104, narrow end of tube held almost straight out.

3. On cake top, pipe tube 104 ruffles following marked curves. Arrange flowers in trios to connect ruffles. Add a flower to each corner of cake at base. Trim with tube 67 leaves. Set birthday candles in ruffled curve. Serves 24.

Fruit and flowers brighten
Birthday cakes for grandparents

Grandma's favorite flower

She'll marvel at this bouquet of ruffled petunias arranged in a white wicker basket.

1. Pipe the petunias in royal icing with tube 102 in a 1⅝" lily nail. Center with a tube 14 green star, then a cluster of tube 1 yellow dots. The quick way to achieve the varied pink tints is to start with light pink icing. Add more color to the icing for deep pink flowers. After piping these flowers, add still more color for crimson petunias. Pipe two circles with tube 8 for handles.

2. Fill a cake baked in the Ball pan. Chill the cake, then form the basket as diagram shows.

3. Cover the cake with basket weaving. Use tube 4 for vertical lines, being careful to keep them straight. Tube 16 weaves the horizontal strokes. Finish top edge with a tube 16 rope border. Attach handles with icing.

4. Mound icing at top of basket and arrange petunias. Fill in with tube 67 leaves. Add a ribboned birthday card, then set tapers around the basket. Serve to ten, adding a petunia to each serving.

A basket of peaches

A luscious birthday tribute to dear Grandpa!

1. Pipe handle in royal icing. Make an arch pattern, 7½" wide at base, 6½" high. Tape wax paper over it. Lay a toothpick at each end of arch. Cover with a tube 8 rope. Dry, then turn over and repeat piping. Dry again.

2. Bake a 6" round layer and one in an 8" Bevel pan. Also bake six Egg mini-cakes for peaches. Ice top of 6" cake, then assemble with bevel cake. Ice peaches in buttercream, then cover with poured fondant. For the pretty "blush", mix food color with two teaspoons of vodka or other white liquor. Paint on peaches with an artist's brush. The vodka will make the blush dry very quickly.

3. Cover cake with basket weaving, using tube 8 for vertical lines, tube 48 for horizontal strokes. Arrange peaches on top of basket and add a gift card and bow. Fill in with tube 70 leaves. Serve the basket to eight—peaches make six additional servings.

Ripe strawberries

Make them in marzipan for delicious berries at any season. Page 35 tells you the easy way to shape them. The graceful oval cake is a pretty background.

1. Pipe royal icing strawberry blossoms with tube 102. The flower is formed just like a wild rose. Add tube 1 stamens.

2. Bake and fill a two-layer oval cake. Ice with buttercream, then cover with poured fondant. Write birthday message with tube 1.

3. Pipe lavish shells at base of cake with tube 4B. Trim each shell with a tube 102 ruffle. Now arrange the berries, securing with dots of icing. Frame the cake with birthday candles in push-in holders. Present this luxurious little masterpiece to Grandma. Serve to twelve, giving each guest a berry.

Happy Birthday!

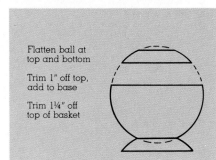

Flatten ball at top and bottom

Trim 1" off top, add to base

Trim 1¼" off top of basket

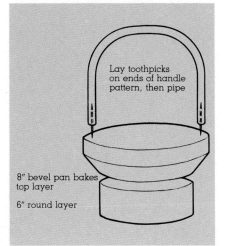

Lay toothpicks on ends of handle pattern, then pipe

8" bevel pan bakes top layer

6" round layer

 is for Christmas . . . <u>Candy</u>, <u>Cookies</u> and <u>Cakes</u> to make and bake and decorate...and for a marvelous Centerpiece <u>Castle</u>!

A Christmas castle

Get your family and friends together—they'll have fun building this never-before gingerbread castle!

Before you begin, gather everything you need for this grand project. Have at hand ingredients for two recipes of gingerbread (page 86), hard candy and boiled and royal icing. You'll also need ice cream cones, a miniature Soldier band and a selection of candies for trim. Purchase three electrical receptacles and three 15-watt bulbs for lighting.

Bake pieces, prepare base

1. Work with one-fourth of the gingerbread recipe at a time, keeping the rest tightly wrapped in plastic. Lightly oil the back of a cookie sheet, lay it on a damp towel to prevent slipping and roll out gingerbread. Dust your rolling pin lightly with flour. Using Celebrate! Holiday Patterns, cut out pieces accurately as possible with a sharp knife. After baking, cool on racks, then lay on paper towels to dry overnight.

2. For "window glass", lay a length of foil, shiny side up, on the back of a cookie sheet or on your marble slab. Lightly brush with oil. Press miniature cutters on the foil to define shapes for windows. You will need about 14 diamonds and 14 hearts, eight circles. Make a recipe of Little lollipops (page 34). With a spoon, cover shapes on foil with candy, letting it spread in irregular fashion about ¼" or more beyond shapes. Let harden, then cover closely with plastic wrap.

3. Make a strong double base for your castle. Lower base is a 22" circle of triple-thick corrugated cardboard, taped together and covered with foil. Glue six stud plates to underside, to form "legs" for base. Upper base is a 20" circle of 1" thick styrofoam. Ice smoothly with royal icing, then attach to lower base with strokes of icing. Using patterns, mark "floor plan" of castle on base. With a sharp knife, cut a 1½" circle out of center of each hexagon on floor plan. Electrical wire will extend through these holes. Attach gingerbread bases with icing. Following diagram, "electrify" the base.

Decorate in royal icing

First lay patterns on baked pieces and trim as necessary with repeated strokes of a sharp knife.

1. Attach "window glass". On wrong side of walls, pipe a tube 2 line around window opening. Press on prepared window. Dry.

2. Attach "awnings" above diamond-shaped windows with royal icing. Pipe freehand trim around all windows with tube 1.

3. Paint ice cream cones with thinned icing. Also paint round cookies that serve as bases below cones. Glue ribbon banner to plastic stick.

Put it all together

Use royal icing, tinted to match gingerbread, as "glue".

1. Do main tower first. Pipe a tube 5 line around two adjacent sides of gingerbread hexagon base. Set one wall against base and pipe a line of icing down side. Pipe icing on side of second wall and join to first. Continue until six walls are in place. Pipe a line of icing on top of assembled walls and gently press on roof. Build turret on top of roof, then complete structure.

2. Construct two smaller towers in same way. Start with walls that attach to main tower. Complete piping trim, then attach candies.

3. Make a recipe of boiled icing for "snow", swirl over upper base and immediately sprinkle with edible glitter. Mark walkway with spatula and press in candies. Pipe a line of royal icing on base of each fence section and gently press in position. Add more snow to roofs and awnings. Arrange soldier band.

To store your castle, roll down the sides of a large, lightweight plastic bag. Set the castle in the bag, gently pull up sides and seal with a twist tie. Now box the castle in a sturdy cardboard carton.

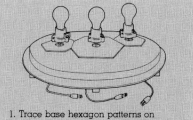

1. Trace base hexagon patterns on upper base for floor plan. Cut out circles from double base. Attach gingerbread hexagon bases with icing.

2. Secure electric receptacles to base.

3. Pass cords through holes in base.

4. Screw in bulbs, plug to test.

Candy from your kitchen! The gift that's sure to please

Candy is fun to make—and homemade candy is more delicious than any you can buy! You'll make it with love and care and the very finest of ingredients.

All the recipes that follow are from *The Complete Wilton Book of Candy.* All of them are for tried and true favorites that delight everyone. We've added some time-saving methods and colorful trims that make them even more appealing for gifts.

For presentation, dress up your candies in their holiday best. Heap them in colorful containers, frill the boxes with paper lace cut from doilies, add ribbon bows.

So follow the easy step-by-step recipes. Discover the thrill of fine candy making—and give your friends the pleasure of truly deluxe treats.

Clockwise, starting top left: Holiday popcorn balls, Deluxe caramel corn, Little lollipops, Molded greeting card, Santa and Snowman figures, Marzipan strawberries, a choice of Pralines, Fondant-dipped apricots, Chocolate mints and Florenettes.

For recipes, please turn the page

Holiday popcorn balls

12 cups freshly popped corn
8 ounces candied cherries,
 chopped
1 cup granulated sugar
1 cup light corn syrup
½ cup water
2 tablespoons butter
2 teaspoons vanilla

Before you begin, chop the cherries with a scissors dipped occasionally in cold water. Butter a large heat-proof bowl, place the popped corn in it, add chopped cherries and mix with your hands. Put bowl in oven set at lowest temperature to warm. Remove bowl when ready to mix with cooked syrup. Line a cookie sheet with wax paper.

1. Combine sugar, syrup and water in a three-quart heavy saucepan. Add butter, cut in thin slices.

Place over medium heat and stir with a wooden spoon until all sugar crystals are dissolved. Wash down sides of pan with a pastry brush dipped in hot water.

Clip on thermometer and continue cooking until temperature reaches 240°F. Remove from heat and stir in vanilla.

2. Pour syrup over the warmed popcorn and toss with two forks until corn is evenly coated. When mixture is cool enough to handle, butter your hands and form into balls about 2½" in diameter. Place on prepared cookie sheet to harden at room temperature. Wrap each ball in a square of plastic wrap, secure with a ribbon. Store for months at room temperature. Yield: 13 to 15 balls.

Deluxe Caramel corn

The very best you've ever tasted! This candy keeps and travels well so it's a much-appreciated gift.

5 cups freshly popped corn
1 cup dry roasted salted
 cashews
1 cup dark corn syrup
1 cup granulated sugar

¼ cup water
¼ cup butter

Before you begin, butter two 12" x 18" cookie sheets. Combine popped corn and cashews in a large buttered heat-proof mixing bowl and place in oven set on lowest temperature. Remove when ready to mix with cooked syrup.

1. Combine corn syrup, sugar and water in a heavy three-quart saucepan. Add butter, cut in thin slices. Place pan on medium heat and stir constantly with a wooden spoon until mixture comes to a boil. Wash down sides of pan with a pastry brush dipped in hot water. Clip on thermometer. Continue cooking, stirring occasionally until temperature reaches 280°F. Remove from heat.

2. Pour over warmed popcorn mixture in bowl. Toss quickly with two forks until nuts and popcorn are well coated. Spread out on prepared cookie sheets. Butter your hands and press into thin layers. Cool about 30 minutes, then break into clusters. Store at room temperature for up to several months in tightly sealed plastic bag. Yield: seven cups.

A lollipop centerpiece

In just a few minutes turn out perfect little lollipops—bright and shiny as jewels! Then arrange them like a bouquet for a good-to-eat centerpiece. Cook in a heavy saucepan.

1 cup granulated cane sugar
⅓ cup hot water
⅓ cup light corn syrup
a few drops liquid food color
½ teaspoon oil-based flavoring
10 small lollipop molds
10 paper lollipop sticks

Before you begin, oil the molds and assemble with sticks on a cookie sheet.

1. Combine sugar, hot water and corn syrup in a heavy one- or two-quart saucepan. Place on high heat and stir with a wooden spoon until all sugar crystals are

disssolved. Wash down sides of pan with a pastry brush dipped in hot water. Clip on thermometer. Continue cooking, without stirring until thermometer registers 300°F, then remove from heat. Cooking takes about nine minutes.

2. Let stand for two minutes until bubbles disappear. Add flavoring and food color and stir to blend. Pour into prepared molds. Let harden at room temperature about ten minutes. Unmold by pressing back of molds lightly. Lay on a paper towel to absorb oil. Wrap each lollipop in clear plastic wrap. Store at room temperature for up to six weeks. Yield: about ten lollipops, about 2" in diameter.

Decorate the lollipops with tube 1 and a mixture of half royal icing, half piping gel. Wedge a piece of styrofoam into a container. Cover with royal icing, insert sticks.

An edible Christmas card

A greeting and a gift in one! Mold this Candy Melts™ confection in a plastic mold, adding bright contrast with the easy Flow-in method. Present to a delighted friend!

The Flow-in method of adding color contrast

This is the quick, neat professional way to give the magic of color to your molded pieces. Here's how we did the greeting card.

1. Melt the two contrasting colors in small glass jars set in a pan of hot water. Place a few white wafers in each jar. Stir until melted, then add candy color, a little at a time, until you achieve the tints you want.

2. Make a small parchment paper cone and fit with tube 1. Use a spoon to fill the cone with red coating, no more than one-third full. Now, with light pressure, fill the "MERRY" and the holly berry indentations of the mold. The cone will allow you to guide the color accurately. Do not overfill the indentations. Allow to set just a few minutes until firm.

3. Do the same with a separate cone and melted green coating to flow in "CHRISTMAS" and leaves. In a few minutes, when coating is firm, fill the mold with melted chocolate-flavored coating. You will need about a half pound. Drop mold sharply on surface several times to remove air bubbles. Place in freezer about 20 minutes to harden, then unmold.

4. To sign the card, spoon a little melted green coating into a small parchment cone fitted with tube 1 or with a tiny cut tip. Practice the letters on a piece of paper to make sure coating is correct consistency. You may need to wait a few minutes for the coating to thicken before writing.

It is most efficient to add contrast to several pieces at a time. Do them in assembly line fashion, color by color.

How to mold Santa and his snowman friend

The Flow-in method is just as quick and easy for two-piece molds. Work with one half of the mold at a time.

1. For Santa, first flow in his chocolate-flavored eyes and boots, let harden, then flow in all white areas. Next flow in red mouth, suit and cap. To check if you have built up sufficient thickness on larger red areas, hold the clear mold up to the light. If you can see light through the red areas, go back and flow in more coating. When this has firmed, clip the two halves of the mold together and fill with melted pink coating. You will need about five ounces. Put in freezer for about 30 minutes, then unmold.

2. For snowman, first flow in buttons, broom handle and eyes, then green hat band, next red mouth, scarf and hat. You may flow in red coating right over the green hat band. Last do the yellow broom. Clip mold together and fill with white coating. The snowman will harden in the freezer in about 30 minutes. Unmold.

A box of strawberries

Red, ripe strawberries make a tempting gift! They're fun to model by hand from delicious marzipan.

Use the recipe on page 85, knead in red liquid food color, then follow these quick, easy steps.

1. Cut off about a third of finished Wilton Basic Marzipan. (Keep remainder well covered.) This amount will make eight or ten strawberries. Dust a cutting board or marble slab with confectioners' sugar. Now roll the tinted marzipan with your hands into a basic cylinder about 1" in diameter. Cut the cylinder into 1½" pieces and form balls by rolling between your palms. Shape each ball into a rounded cone by rolling again between the heels of your hands. Set aside to harden.

2. When shapes are firm, moisten by rolling over a damp sponge or paper towel. Immediately roll in crystal sugar. (Tint sugar by working in liquid food color with your fingers.)

3. Tint a small amount of marzipan green and roll out as thin as possible. Cut shapes with the calyx cutter (from the Flower garden set). Curl points with a modeling stick, brush a little egg white on center of back and press to berry. Roll a little string of green marzipan, let harden for a few minutes, then cut ½" lengths for stems. Dip end in egg white and attach to finished berry. Brush calyxes and stems with Corn syrup glaze, then dry. Put each luscious berry in a candy cup and arrange in a lace-trimmed box.

Corn syrup glaze

   ½ cup light corn syrup
   1 cup water

Combine syrup and water and heat to boiling in a small saucepan. Brush on marzipan pieces while hot. Allow pieces to dry at room temperature, about 20 minutes. This will give a soft shine.

Pralines, enticing nut-filled candies are a treat for anyone. Here are pralines in blonde and brunette versions. They're formed in round candy molds for a neat, professional look.

Butterscotch pralines

Here is the enticing blonde of the praline family. Crisp almonds give a delicate crunch, sour cream a fascinating tang.

   1 cup light brown sugar, lightly packed
   1 cup granulated sugar
   ½ cup dairy sour cream
   2 tablespoons butter
   pinch of salt
   1 cup sliced almonds, crisped
   ½ teaspoon butterscotch flavoring

Before you begin, crisp the almonds. Preheat oven to 300°F, spread nuts on cookie sheet and place in oven. Turn off heat. Remove in ten minutes. Lightly butter two cookie sheets. Butter inner surfaces of round candy molds and arrange on cookie sheets.

1. Combine sugars, cream, butter (cut in thin slices) and salt in a three-quart heavy saucepan. Put on medium-low heat, stirring constantly until mixture comes to a boil. Wash down sides of pan with a pastry brush dipped in hot water and clip on thermometer. Stirring occasionally, cook until thermometer registers 236°F. Remove from heat. Entire cooking time will be about 25 to 30 minutes.

2. Immediately add nuts and flavoring. Stir briefly, just until mixture begins to thicken—then drop by tablespoon into prepared candy molds. If mixture becomes too thick, stir in one or two teaspoons of hot water. Cool at room temperature about 30 minutes. Wrap each patty in plastic wrap. Place in a tightly sealed plastic bag to store for a month at room temperature. Yield: 24 pralines.

Continued on page 42

Sparkling Christmas decor to make yourself

Leaf through the next few pages. More enchanting than any you could buy—all these bright ornaments are fashioned from gum paste! You and your family will have fun making them—and they're really easy to do. If you can roll out cookies, you can fashion these trims!

Wilton gum paste

Make this recipe the day before you plan to make the ornaments.
- 1 tablespoon Gum-tex™ or tragacanth gum
- 1 heaping tablespoon glucose
- 3 tablespoons warm water
- 1 pound confectioners' sugar (or more)

Heat glucose and water till just warm. Mix Gum-tex with 1 cup of the sugar and add to glucose mixture. Mix well. Gradually knead in enough sugar until you have used about ¾ pound.

Gum paste handles best when aged, so store in a tightly closed plastic bag at least overnight, then break off a piece and work in more sugar until pliable but not sticky. Always keep well-covered.

To store for months, place gum paste in a plastic bag and then in a covered container to prevent drying.

To tint, apply a little paste food color with a toothpick. Knead to spread tint evenly.

To roll out gum paste, dust your work surface well with cornstarch. Work a small piece of gum paste and roll it out with a small rolling pin, also dusted with cornstarch.

Christmas angel lights

1. Tint a small amount of gum paste yellow for hair. Divide the rest of the recipe in thirds. Tint one portion green, one red and leave the remainder untinted. Make green frames and angels separately. For frames, roll out gum paste about ⅛" thick. Cut a 2" x 13" strip. Wrap this around your styrofoam block as diagram shows. Wrap around the block, meeting at back. Trim so seam butts, and brush a little egg white on seam to fasten. While gum paste is wet, cut a pointed curve in center of each side, about 1" x 1½" deep. Cut holes with tube 8. Dry.

2. For angel, roll out untinted gum paste ⅛" thick. Cut out with the angel Christmas cutter. Immediately, cut a second angel from red rolled gum paste. Trim off wings, hands and head. Brush white angel with egg white and place red dress on her. Cut a little curve from yellow rolled gum paste for hair. Brush edge of head with egg white and lay hair on head. Finally cut a star with a Miniature cutter and attach to head with egg white. Working while gum paste is still wet, cut holes in the angel, using round tubes and tube 79 for mouth. Dry.

3. Attach an angel to each side of frame. Lay frame on side. Form several tiny balls of wet gum paste. Flatten, dip in egg white and place between angel and frame. Let first angel set up before attaching second. Set a vigil light within each frame. One recipe of gum paste will make two angels. Spray them with clear acrylic glaze and they will last for years.

6" x 3" styrofoam block wrapped with wax paper

Wrap 2" strip of gum paste around block

Cut out curves with knife. Cut holes with tube. Dry

Christmas mobile of butterflies and birds

See page 40 for directions

Sweet Victorian
Christmas ornaments

See page 40 for directions

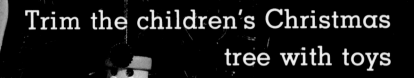

Trim the children's Christmas
tree with toys

See page 40 for directions

Directions for gum paste Christmas trims

Gum paste, rolled out just like cookie dough, makes these charming ornaments. Use the recipe on page 36, and tint. Cut out the shapes with cutters, tubes or *Celebrate!* patterns.

1. Put pieces together two ways. *If one or both pieces are wet,* brush with egg white and gently press together. Dry thoroughly. *If both pieces are dry,* form a little ball of wet gum paste, flatten, dip in egg white and lay on piece. Gently press second piece to it, then dry.

2. Add sparkle with sequins and glitter to finished ornaments. Attach with white household glue.

3. Spray all ornaments twice with acrylic glaze. This adds a nice gloss, and seals out moisture.

Butterflies and birds, *page 37*

1. *For birds,* use patterns to cut wings and bodies from gum paste rolled ⅛" thick. Dry bodies flat, wings within largest curved surface. Attach one wing and dry. Lay bird on top of glass, wing inside, then attach second wing. Prop wings with cotton balls while drying. Glue on sequins.

2. *For butterflies, cut out wings* with pattern. Form designs by cutting holes with tubes or truffle cutters. Dry on 8" curved former. Glue on sequins. Pipe body with royal icing and tube 9 on wax paper. Insert wings into body and prop with cotton balls. Cut antennae from fine copper wire and insert. Bend one end of a wire into hook and insert in body. Dry.

Victorian ornaments, *page 38*

1. *Flat stars, hearts and angels.* Cut with cookie cutters, then add "appliques" cut with truffle cutters. Cut hole for hanging with tube 3. Dry flat. Add sequins and cord.

2. *Dimensional stars.* Cut a star with a cookie cutter, then cut a ⅛" slit from center to top of star. Cut a second star with same cutter, and cut slit from center to bottom. Dry both stars flat. Trim with sequins. Slip the two stars together. Glue.

3. *Fans.* Cut flowers and leaves with the violet and small rose leaf cutters from the Flower garden set. Follow directions in set. Twist all stems together. Fold an 8" gold paper doily in half, then pleat. Push stems through hole in doily and hook. Add bow.

4. *Cornucopia.* Cut out with pattern. Cover a tree former with wax paper and wrap gum paste shape around it, butting seam at back. When dry, attach contrasting trims cut with truffle cutters and glue on sequins. Fill with candies or flowers.

5. *Cupid.* Mold angelino from flesh colored gum paste in Baroque mold, following directions with mold. Hook end of a 6" wire and insert wire in back at forehead level. Dry over 6" curved former. Brush with powdered chalk. Glue two 4" gold paper doilies together, back to back. Pleat, then draw wire through hole in center of doily. Glue on sequins.

Toy ornaments, *page 39*

1. *Boys, girls and clowns* are all cut with Christmas cutters. Trim with "appliques" cut with truffle and miniature cutters. Cut features with round tubes. Cut hole for hanging, dry. Add sequins.

2. *Drums.* Cut top and bottom with a 2½" round cutter. Glue gold cord for hanging to back of top and dry flat. For side of drum, tape wax paper around a paste color jar. Cut a 1¾" x 6¾" strip of green gum paste and wrap around jar, trimming and butting seam. Dry. Glue on gold cord in "V's". Glue top and bottom to side. Cut a ¼" x 8" strip of yellow gum paste, brush with egg white and wrap around top of drum. Repeat for bottom. Glue on sequins. Drum sticks are toothpicks inserted into red balls.

3. *Rocking horses.* Cut two shapes for each horse, following pattern, and dry as shown in diagram in pattern book. Cut out rockers, brush with egg white and attach. On one horse-shape, glue on gold cord for mane and tail. Put two horses together. Cut out saddle, brush with egg white and attach. Add a little string of red gum paste for mouth and glue on sequins.

4. *Sled.* Following patterns, cut runners first from ⅛" thick gum paste and dry flat. Cut top, brush outer edges with egg white and prop runners on it in upside down position. Dry, then glue on sequin.

5. *Soldier.* Start with a two-ounce liquid food color bottle! Tape wax paper smoothly over both cap and cover. Cut a strip of untinted gum paste the height of the bottle and about 4¼" long. Wrap around bottle, trimming seam in back. Groove in center front for trouser legs. Cut a 1½" x 4¼" strip of red gum paste, brush with egg white and wrap around upper part of bottle. Wrap a strip of flesh-colored gum paste around cover for head. Wrap top of head with a ¼" strip of red gum paste for hat. Dry and remove from bottle. Cut a red and a white circle with a 1¼" cutter and attach to top and bottom of larger cylinder. Cut a 1" circle of red gum paste for top of hat. Make a hole in the center, insert a wire loop for hanging and dry. Attach to top of head, attach head to body. Form two cylinders, 1⅛" x ¼" thick, for arms. Attach with egg white. Belt is a ¼" strip, beard is a fringed fan shape trimmed from a 1½" circle, epaulets are cut with the base of a standard tube and fringed, hands are cut with tube 2A and feet from the same tube, shaped to a point at back. Round tubes cut cheeks and mouth. Add sequins.

A candle-lit Cookie centerpiece

Get out your sets of Star and Round cookie cutters to create this holiday centerpiece. You will need two recipes of the Roll-out cookies (page 85). Tint the dough a delicate green.

1. For the large tree, cut two of each of the ten sizes of stars in the set. Roll out and cut on a flat cookie sheet, then pick up scraps. Fill a parchment cone with crystal sugar, cut the tip and sprinkle

points of stars with the sugar. No mess! Check after ten minutes baking—do not allow edges to brown. Cut a hole for candle in one of the smallest stars. Bake also two cookies cut with each size of the Round cutter set plus two cut with top of tube 1A and base of tube 190.

2. Cover a 16" double cake board with foil, attach a triple 14" board and heap with boiled icing.

Assemble trees on board.

3. For tallest tree, stack the cookies with strokes of icing, placing first a star cookie, then a round as separator. For smallest tree, use only the four smallest star cutters. For medium tree, use the seven smallest cutters. Build just as for large tree.

41

New Orleans deluxe pralines

This candy is crowded with crisp pecan halves, has a creamy delicate grain and a rich caramel flavor. Very quick and easy!

1 cup dark brown sugar, lightly packed
1 cup granulated sugar
⅔ cup evaporated milk, undiluted
½ teaspoon vanilla extract
2 cups pecan halves, roasted

Before you begin, roast the pecans. Spread on a cookie sheet and place in a preheated 350°F oven for about eight minutes. Stir frequently for even browning. Use no butter or oil. Butter inner surfaces of round candy molds and place on cookie sheets.

1. Combine sugars and milk in a heavy three-quart saucepan. Place over medium heat and stir constantly with a wooden spoon until all sugar crystals are dissolved. Wash down sides of pan with a pastry brush dipped in hot water, then clip on thermometer. Turn heat to medium-low and continue cooking to 236°F. Entire cooking time is about 25 to 30 minutes. Remove from heat.

2. Add vanilla and nuts and stir briefly, just until nuts are well coated and mixture becomes a little lighter. Immediately drop from tablespoon into prepared molds. If mixture becomes too stiff to drop, stir in one or two teaspoons of hot water. Cool at room temperature until firm, about 30 minutes. Wrap individually in plastic wrap. To store for a month, place in a tightly sealed plastic bag. Yield: about 27 pralines.

Fondant-dipped apricots

Turn dried apricots into decorative and elegant sweets by dipping in fondant. The creamy fondant softens and sweetens the intense flavors of the fruit.

30 dried apricots
2 cups Wilton quick fondant, tinted green (page 84)
1 cup Chocolate quick fondant

1. Prepare fruit. Steam over simmering water for about 15 minutes to soften and plump.

2. Dip 15 apricots in green-tinted fondant first. Holding fruit by one side, dip in fondant, covering only half of fruit. Lay on wax paper for fondant to set, only about ten minutes. Dip 15 apricots in chocolate fondant the same way. Now go back and dip green fondant-dipped fruit a second time.

Place each apricot in a paper candy cup, then arrange in candy box. Cover tightly with clear plastic wrap, then cover box. Store for a week in a cool place. Yield: 30 dipped apricots.

Chocolate mints are everybody's favorite! Here is the easy recipe for the centers.

Uncooked butter fondant

A rich and delicious fondant for centers that can be put together in about 15 minutes.

⅓ cup butter
¼ teaspoon salt
⅓ cup light corn syrup
¼ teaspoon peppermint extract
1 pound sifted confectioners' sugar (approximate)
1 pound confectionery coating, chocolate flavor

Before you begin, line two cookie sheets with wax paper. Lightly dust with flour.

1. Whip butter and salt in electric mixer set at medium speed until fluffy. Use large bowl of mixer. Add corn syrup in thirds, whipping after each addition. Add peppermint extract.

2. Add sugar, all at once, and stir with a wooden spoon until mixture holds together. Turn out on a surface very lightly dusted with flour. Knead until perfectly smooth and can be formed into a ball.

3. Divide fondant into halves and work with one portion at a time. Lightly dust a smooth surface and your rolling pin with flour. Roll out to about ⅛" thickness and cut circles with mold. Lay on prepared cookie sheet. Sprinkle lightly with flour. Knead scraps into remainder of fondant, roll out and cut as before. Allow centers to crust at room temperature overnight. To store for two weeks, wrap ball of fondant tightly in two layers of plastic wrap and refrigerate. Bring to room temperature to roll out. Yield: about 30 centers.

To dip centers, first cover the backs of two cookie sheets with wax paper and lightly dust with flour.

1. Melt the confectionery coating. Fill lower pan of a two-quart double boiler with water to a depth below level of top pan. Bring to a simmer, then remove from heat. Put coating in top pan and set in position on lower pan. Stir constantly, do not beat, until coating is smooth and completely melted. Check temperature. Unless you are very experienced in melting coating, we recommend using a thermometer. For thorough melting, the coating should be brought to 110°F, never higher than 115°F. When it reaches 110°F, remove top pan from lower pan, dry the outside, and stir until thermometer registers from 95°F to 100°F. Pan will be just warm.

2. Brush excess flour from centers. Set centers to left of pan, prepared cookie sheet to right of pan. Use a dipping fork with widely spaced tines.

3. Allow dipped mints to firm at room temperature, about 15 minutes. Use a rubber scraper to scrape remaining coating from pan onto a length of foil. Let harden, then store in tightly sealed plastic bag.

Continued on page 47

Cute little cakes for Christmas

For directions, please turn the page

43

Build a Christmas house from cake

Just as cute as a gingerbread house and even more delicious!

Mold candy trims in advance

1. Assemble all you need to create this centerpiece. Windows, shutters, chimney, door and doorstep are molded in the square candy mold. Small tree molds and tree lollipop molds are used to landscape the lawn. Add a round mint mold and a small heart mold to finish the door. Miniature pretzels form the fence. Small chocolate-covered candies and candy canes complete the trim.

2. Mold all the shapes in Candy Melts™ confectionery coating. Dip the pretzels in chocolate-flavored confectionery coating.

Bake, ice and assemble

3. Bake a two-layer cake in a 10" square pan for lawn. The house itself is baked in the house pan. One cake mix makes the front of the house, a second mix is baked in the same pan for the back.

4. Fill the 10" layers, chill, ice in buttercream and set on foil-covered cake board. Secure the front to the back of the house with icing and level base. Set on its own cardboard cake base, cut same size and shape as the house. Insert a circle of six ¼" dowel rods in the center of the 10" cake and clip off level with top. This will support the house cake. Ice house in chocolate buttercream and set on 10" cake. Pipe holly leaves with tube 67, pull out points with a damp brush, freeze or air-dry.

Decorate the centerpiece

5. Pipe a tube 10 ball border at base of 10" cake. Pipe message with tube 2. Do "eaves" at top of cake house with tube 2B. Attach small chocolate-covered candies with icing for foundation. Attach all molded candies except free-standing trees with dots of icing. Define window panes with tube 1.

6. Make a batch of boiled icing, thin with corn syrup and swirl over roof, pulling out "icicles" with a small spatula. Do the same for "yard". Immediately sprinkle with edible glitter.

7. Add finishing touches. Attach holly leaves with dots of icing and pipe red berries with tube 3. Plant lollipop trees in yard. Make the path with small chocolate covered candies, then build the fence with the dipped pretzels, attaching each on a little mound of icing. Press two candy canes into each corner of base cake and trim with ribbon bows. Stroke a little more icing "snow" on fence and trees and sprinkle immediately with edible glitter. Your cozy little holiday house is finished! Serve house to 24, base cake to 20.

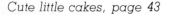

Cute little cakes, page 43

Children love anything miniature—and especially sweet treats baked just for them.

Santa's elves

Start with their favorite cake baked in the Egg minicake pan. Each elf is a half-egg. Ice the cakes with buttercream, making it smooth as possible. Set the cakes on a rack over a cookie sheet and cover with Quick poured fondant.

Now add their jaunty caps and cheerful features. Use tube 3 to pipe smiles, nose and bright eyes (flatten with a cornstarched finger). For rosy cheeks, add just a bit of water to liquid food color and paint with an artist's brush.

Fill in area of caps with tube 16 stars, then add tube 3 spiky hair. The pompon on hat is a gum-drop.

Arrange on a serving tray and watch the smiles!

Jolly snowmen

These bright little creatures start with the Egg minicake pan again. Each is made of two halves, filled and fastened with toothpicks. Trim a little off the broad end of the eggs so they stand securely.

Ice the egg shapes, then rough up with a damp sponge. For heads, impale marshmallows on toothpicks, dip in thinned icing, then rough with a sponge. Stick into a styrofoam block to dry.

Now bring the cakes to life. Trim curves off small candy canes and insert in egg shapes for arms. Pipe tube 104 scarves on eggs, then stick in prepared marshmallows. Add features with tube 3, hats with tube 8B upright stars. The buttons are "red hot" candies.

Here's Santa himself!

A Mini-Santa pan makes it easy to produce these portraits. Bake the cakes, chill, then ice smoothly with buttercream. Let icing set, then place cakes on rack over a cookie sheet and cover with Quick poured fondant. (If fondant does not cover cap and beard area, don't be disturbed. These areas will be covered with piping.)

Use food color diluted with a few drops of water and an artist's brush to give color to Santa's cheeks and nose. Pipe mouth and eyes with tube 3. Pipe curving mustache with tube 17.

Tube 14 does all the rest of the decorating. Pull out strands for beard, curves for eyebrows, stars for cap and zigzags for cap brim. Finish off with a jaunty pompon.

Christmas gifts from your kitchen

Quick & Pretty

A festive fruit cake

Take just a little time to add delicious marzipan trim to your cake. The recipe on page 86 makes three loaves, about 3½" x 7½".

1. The marzipan recipe on page 85 will be enough to trim three cakes. Divide into halves. Tint one half green. Divide the remaining marzipan into halves. Tint one half red—leave the other untinted.

2. Form a cylinder of the green marzipan. Roll out about ⅛" thick and the length of the circumference of your cake. Lightly roll over again with a grooved rolling pin. Cut into a strip the height of the cake. Brush light corn syrup on the side of cake and wrap the strip around it. Cut leaves with the holly leaf Flower garden cutter.

Roll out untinted marzipan and cut a strip 1" x 4" for the candle. Slant top edge. From rolled red marzipan, cut flame with Flower garden small violet leaf cutter, berries with tube 2A. For candle holder, cut a 1" x 2½" strip and slant the ends. Brush top of cake with hot, light corn syrup and assemble candle. Brush again with the hot syrup. Add lace paper strips and a ribbon.

Quick & Pretty

A popcorn tree!

Mold the popcorn in the Tree-lightful pan, trim with candies.

1. Use 14 cups of popped corn and the cooked syrup recipe for Holiday popcorn balls, page 34. Omit cherries. After corn is coated with syrup, press firmly into well-buttered pan. Immediately, turn out on buttered wax paper.

2. Attach candy trim with hot corn syrup. Brush Corn syrup glaze, page 35, over completed tree.

Christmas candy, con'd

To trim the mints, use the Cutout method. It's quick, easy and gives a very pretty finish to the candies. Tiny truffle cutters form the shapes.

1. Cover the back of a cookie sheet with foil, shiny side up. Tape to secure. Melt about a quarter pound of red-tinted confectionery coating according to directions page 42. Spread the coating smoothly over the foil with a large spatula, keeping the coating about 1/16" thick.

2. Wait until the confectionery coating has set up but not completely hardened. If your work area is 72°F, this will take about 5 minutes. Cut the shapes with a truffle cutter just as you would cut out cookies, pressing the cutter firmly through the coating. For circles, use a round decorating tube. Cut out shapes from green-tinted coating the same way.

3. Allow coating to harden completely, about ten minutes at room temperature. Remove tape and slide your hand gently beneath foil. Cut-out shapes will pop up. Attach cut-outs to mints with dots of melted coating. Save scraps to melt again.

Florenettes

The very best fruit-nut candy! This easy-to-make adaptation of an old European recipe has an intriguing flavor and a delicate crispness. Use round stainless steel molds to form the candies.

¼ cup butter
15 large marshmallows, quartered
½ teaspoon almond flavoring
½ cup chopped candied orange peel
¼ cup chopped candied cherries
1 cup slivered almonds, crisped
½ pound tempered milk or dark chocolate. Or use confectionery coating, chocolate flavored.

Before you begin, chop and measure the orange peel and cherries. Chopping is easiest

done with a scissors dipped in cold water. Cut marshmallows in quarters. To crisp the almonds, preheat oven to 300°F, spread the nuts on a cookie sheet, place in oven and turn off heat. Remove in ten minutes. Line two cookie sheets with foil and brush with vegetable oil. Thoroughly brush inner surfaces of the round molds with oil. Arrange them on the cookie sheets. Preheat oven to 350°F.

1. Melt butter in a two-quart saucepan over lowest heat. Add marshmallows and stir constantly with a wooden spoon until marshmallows are completely melted. Remove from heat and stir in almond flavoring.

2. Add orange peel, cherries and almonds and stir until well blended. Drop by teaspoon into prepared molds. Bake in 350°F oven for ten minutes. As soon as candy is taken from oven lift molds away from candies. Cool candies on cookie sheet about 20 minutes, then remove from cookie sheet with a spatula. Cool completely on baking rack.

3. This final step may be done as soon as candy is completely cool or the next day. Cover flat cookie sheet smoothly with foil, shiny side up. Melt and temper the chocolate as directed on page 143. Spread the bottom of a candy with chocolate, using a small spatula. Turn it over, and press it firmly, chocolate side down, on the cookie sheet. Repeat for all candies. Place cookie sheet in refrigerator for about ten minutes to harden the chocolate. Remove from sheet. Bottoms of candies will be smooth and shiny from being pressed against the foil. Store for up to two weeks in a tightly sealed container in a cool dry place (not the refrigerator). Yield: about 22 Florenettes.

Christmas Angel Cake

A golden haired angel makes a pretty holiday centerpiece. Decoration is done mainly with the quick star technique.

1. Bake a cake in the Christmas angel pan. Ice book, hands, face and feet smoothly as possible. Pipe "Merry Christmas" with tube 1. Fill in side at bottom of cake with tube 16 stars. Pipe hem ruffle with tube 125. Now cover entire area of dress with tube 16 stars. Trim scallops on red robe with tube 13 stars.

2. Figure pipe chubby cheeks with tube 6, eyes with tube 4, mouth with tube 3. Pull out wing feathers with tube 401, starting with lowest ones. Pipe golden hair with tube 16, then add a tube 10 halo. Serve to twelve guests.

A holiday house in candy!

Use Candy Melts™ confectionery coating to mold this little house and its yard, then dress it up for Christmas with flowing curves molded in coating.

1. Melt coating as described on page 42. Fill House molds and place in freezer for about 20 minutes, or until hardened. Unmold. You will need about 1½ pounds of chocolate flavored

coating, ½ pound for pink roof. Mold yard in a 10″ square pan, using about 1½ pounds of white coating.

2. Mold the trims in Baroque molds. Use the shell and fleur-de-lis of Regalia, center oval of Scroll, and Mantle. Use Stars and Shapes mold for the star and corner trim. Cut heart shapes in two. Pipe wreaths on ovals with melted coating and a parchment cone with cut tip.

3. Attach yard to a 12″ foil-covered cake board. Assemble house on yard with melted coating in a parchment cone with cut tip. Pipe a line of coating on base of front wall. Hold in place until set. Pipe coating on one side of front wall, and on base of a side wall. Set in position. Continue until all walls are assembled. Pipe coating on inside of corners to reinforce. When walls are set up, add roof,

one section at a time. Pipe coating on top of walls, then set roof section in position. Hold until set. Finish by piping a line of coating on top ridge of roof.

4. Attach all molded trims with dots of melted coating. Surround yard with purchased chocolate candies. Make a little pattern for walk and cut from coating with the cut-out method, page 47. Shower the scene with Edible glitter.

is for cakes <u>Decorated</u> in foreign styles, the <u>Dainty</u> Australian and <u>Dramatic</u> English Over-piped methods.

Every decorator looks forward to the challenge of decorating in foreign methods. These are the traditional styles on which the Wilton-American way is based. If you are an experienced decorator, you will only be using techniques you already know.

The dainty Australian style is characterized by perfect proportion and delicate detail. Lace, curtaining (similar to our lattice) and embroidery are done meticulously with tiny tubes. Even the flowers, made usually in gum paste, are refined and never over-power the over-all grace of the cake. The cake at right is a beautiful example of the pure Australian style.

Prepare cake and trims

1. Australian cakes are fruit cakes. Covered with marzipan, then rolled fondant, they will remain fresh for weeks. Bake the two-layer cake in oval pans and fill with rolled marzipan. Trim to a level height of 3". Cover the cake as shown on page 52 for a satin-smooth surface. Transfer *Celebrate!* pattern to cake top. Divide cake in twelfths and mark 2⅝" up from base. Transfer curtaining pattern to side of cake, placing point of pattern at marks on cake. Your curtaining will be ⅜" above base of cake.

2. For the gum paste flowers, use the briar rose cutter from the Flower garden set, and the directions that come with it. For super-thin petals, roll out the gum paste on a smooth surface that has been oiled, then wiped off with a paper towel. Cut leaves with the small rose leaf cutter.

Make three poufs from 3" squares of fine tulle. Bunch at center and secure with fine florists' wire. Wire loops of ⅛" ribbon, then twist stems of flowers, leaves, poufs and ribbon into a bouquet. We used three briar roses and three buds.

3. Pipe the lace pieces on wax paper taped over *Celebrate!* patterns. Use Egg white royal icing and tube 0L.

4. Make the oval cake board from two thicknesses of corrugated cardboard cut 2" larger all around than the cake. Cover with foil and edge with a ribbon. Transfer covered and marked cake to the board, attaching with royal icing.

Decorate the cake

Use tiny tubes, Egg white royal icing and careful light pressure for all trims. Thin the icing with additional egg white, if necessary, so it flows easily from the tube.

1. Fill the marked area on cake top with tube 00L cornelli lace—meandering curves that never touch. Do not stop piping until entire area is filled. Edge with tube 0L beading. Pipe a tube 3 bulb border at base of cake.

2. Pipe tube 00L freehand embroidery on cake side—tiny dot flowers, leaves and clusters of dots.

3. Pipe the extension work—tiny shelves that support the curtaining. Use tube 1. First drop a string the full width of the triangle pattern base. Now over-pipe this string with a shorter line. Repeat two more times, making each line shorter, for a total of four lines. After piping two lines on each triangle, *allow to dry* before piping additional lines. When all extensions are dry, pipe a finishing tube 1 line all around curves. Dry, then brush with thinned icing.

4. Do the curtaining—parallel tube 00L dropped strings. Drop center string first from point of marked triangle to center of extension. Then fill in with more strings, spaced very closely.

5. Run a tube 0L "snail's trail" around upper edges of curtaining. This is piped just like a shell border. Finish with spaced dots on cake side. Pipe a dot border with tube 0L at base of curtaining. Pipe four dots, then go back and pipe another dot between last two. Continue around cake.

6. Finally attach lace pieces. Pipe a tiny tube 0L line of icing against bead border. Hold a lace piece to it. Continue around cake top, making sure all lace pieces slant at the same angle. Set bouquet on cake. Your lovely Australian cake is complete! Serve wedding cake-sized pieces to 24 guests.

How to cover cakes Decorated in foreign styles

For Australian cakes, prepare a recipe of marzipan and one of rolled fondant. (Recipes on page 85). For apricot glaze, heat one cup of apricot jam to boiling and strain. Use while hot.

1. Bake a fruitcake, attach a cardboard cake circle and fill holes and crevices with marzipan. Brush cake top and sides with apricot glaze. Dust work surface with confectioners' sugar, then roll out marzipan to a ⅜" thick circle large enough to cover the entire cake. Fold the marzipan over the rolling pin, place on edge of cake and unroll over the cake.

2. Gently press marzipan into place and smooth with palms of hands. Marzipan has no stretch, so if a crack appears, pinch together and rub with palm until smooth. Trim off excess marzipan at base. Let harden at least twelve hours before covering with fondant.

3. Brush marzipan covering with apricot glaze. Coat work surface with non-stick pan release and dust with cornstarch. Roll fondant out to a ¼" thick circle large enough to cover entire cake. Fold the fondant over rolling pin, place on end of cake and unroll. Smooth fondant into place. Trim excess at base, smooth and trim again. Transfer cake to cake board.

For English over-piped cakes, cover first with marzipan before icing with royal icing.

1. Attach a cardboard cake circle onto the top of the cake with royal icing. Pack space between cardboard and cake with marzipan. This is now the bottom of the cake. Fill any holes or cracks with marzipan. Roll out marzipan into a circle ⅜" thick and slightly larger than the cake diameter. Brush the top of the cake with warm apricot glaze. Place cake upside-down on marzipan, cardboard on top. Trim off excess at edge.

2. Shape remaining marzipan into a long narrow roll and flatten. Using a ruler, trim one long side. Brush cake side with apricot glaze. Place cake on its side on strip. Set bottom edge of cake along straight edge of strip and roll, patting marzipan into place. Trim seam so edges butt.

3. Turn cake upright and trim off excess marzipan around top. Press side seam together and smooth. Pat cake all over to smooth. Let harden 48 hours before icing with two thin smooth coats of royal icing. Drying time is needed so almond oil will not discolor icing.

A splendid cake
Decorated in the English Over-piped style

For directions, please turn the page

How to Decorate the English Over-piped cake

The over-piped style has been perfected by many English decorators in the 19th and present centuries. Cakes are of lofty proportions, ornamented by line upon line of accurate, curving over-piping which combine for a dramatic, sculptural effect. Gum paste trims are often used. This style demands a steady, skillful hand, but the results are spectacular, as this wedding cake shows.

Prepare the cake

1. Bake layers of fruit cake in 10" round pans and a cake in the 14" base bevel pan. Use marzipan or apricot glaze as filling. Make sure the assembled 10" layers are exactly 5" high and level. Assemble with bevel cake, then cover with marzipan as shown on page 52. Ice with royal icing, dry thoroughly, then ice again for a perfectly smooth surface.

2. Divide cake into eighths and mark at top edge. Transfer *Celebrate!* pattern for top scroll designs, centering each between marks and keeping outer edges of scrolls at edge of cake top. Transfer center star pattern, placing points in line with marks. Transfer patterns for four hearts, side scrolls and lower curves to side of cake. Divide base of cake into fourths, then 20ths and mark ¾" up from outer edge of bevel, making sure that four spaces are directly below points of lower curves, where angelicas will be placed.

Make trims in advance

1. Mold four angelicas in gum paste, using Baroque molds. Also mold 16 side plumes with the regalia mold and assemble back to back, for eight plumes. When dry, tint angelicas by brushing with shaved pastels. Using the lily and leaf cutters from the Flower garden set, make five gum paste lilies and twelve leaves. Follow directions in the booklets that come with molds and cutters.

2. Pipe about 300 tiny wild roses with royal icing and tube 101s. Add tube 1s centers and dry.

Decorate cake top

All trim is done with royal icing. *Pipe no more than two lines* before letting lines set up, so overpiping does not collapse. As you wait, work on another section of the cake. Place lines accurately, one atop the other.

1. Center star. Pipe *inner line* with tube 2, then 1. *Middle line:* tube 3,2,2 and finally 1. *Outer line:* tube 5,3,3,2 and 1. Add spaced tube 1s dots within star and dots at points.

Scrolls. First outline with tube 16 zigzags, then with a tube 15 line. Add succeeding lines with tube 5,3,3,2 and 1.

Decorate side of cake

1. Pipe side scrolls with tube 4,3,2,2 and 1. Pipe *inner heart* shape with tube 3,2 and 1. *Middle line of heart:* tube 4,3,2,2 and 1. *Outer line of heart:* tube 5,4,4,3,3, 2,2 and 1. Top with tube 1s dots.

2. Do lower curves. *Top line:* tube 3,2 and 1. *Middle line:* tube 4,3,2,2 and 1. *Bottom line:* tube 5,4,4,3,3, 2,2 and 1. Add spaced tube 1s dots and top points with dots.

3. Decorate bevel. Pipe a tube 16 shell border at outer edge. Pipe tube 15 zigzag scallops from mark to mark. Top with a tube 14 line, then a tube 3 line. Add tube 1s dots at points. Pipe tube 352 leaves, points resting on board.

Complete the trim

Pipe a mound of icing in center of cake top and arrange lilies and leaves. Attach gum paste plumes with dots of icing. Set angelicas on bevel on icing mounds. Now attach wild roses and trim with tube 349 leaves. A masterpiece! Serve cake to 98, bevel to 16 wedding guests.

 is for <u>Easter</u> that <u>Enchanting</u> season marked by all the signs of fresh new life— baby animals, blooming flowers and fabulous <u>Easter Eggs!</u>

Bunnies, baby chicks and newborn lambs! Pose these cute little creatures on simple cakes, then add the special treat of molded candy trim. You'll create spectacular Easter centerpieces.

Please turn the page

Two pink bunnies . . .

crouch on a flowery cake. Bodies are baked in Egg minicake pans.

1. Do trims in advance. Pipe royal icing drop flowers with tube 225. Mold six or more flowers in the Daisy mold with Candy Melts™.

2. Make the bunnies. For the pair, you will need four half-eggs of cake. Put halves together with icing, ice with buttercream, and rough with a damp sponge.

Pipe the ears in royal icing. Lay toothpicks on squares of wax paper and pipe long leaf shapes with tube 70 right over them. Lay within curved forms to dry. For head, insert a toothpick into a marshmallow, ice, then roughen with a damp sponge. Stick into styrofoam to dry.

3. Assemble bunny on wax paper. Pipe two front paws with tube 12. Use the same tube for back legs. First pipe paw, then upper part of leg on side of body, as a large shell shape. Pull out fluffy tail with tube 14. Insert toothpick to attach head, then ears. Pipe features with tube 3 and a mixture of half piping gel, half royal icing.

4. Decorate the cake. Bake, fill and ice a two-layer 7″ x 9″ oval cake. Do all the quick decorating with tube 68. Pipe shell motion borders and ruffled garlands. Attach daisies with icing and trim with leaves. Set bunnies on top of cake, add drop flowers and ribbon bows. Serve the cake to twelve.

Chirping chicks

What could be springier than these fluffy yellow pets!

1. Mold pastel eggs for trim in confectionery coating.

2. Make chicks. Bodies are two half-eggs (baked in the Egg minicake pan) put together with icing, then iced with buttercream. Roughen with a damp sponge.

For head, insert a toothpick in a marshmallow, ice with buttercream and roughen surface with sponge. Insert toothpick into body. Pipe topknots, fluffy wings and tails with tube 401. Blue eyes are tube 3, beaks tube 349.

3. Bake, fill and ice a two-layer 8″ round cake. Divide cake side into eighths and mark 1″ up from base. Pipe a bottom shell border with tube 16. Drop guidelines, then pipe tube 18 garlands. Trim with tube 14 stars at points. Pipe tube 16 puff garlands at top edge. Set chicks on cake, then pull up grass with tube 233. Serve cake to ten .

Two little lambs

These adorable little pets are easy to put together from marsh-mallows and toothpicks.

1. Mold Candy Melts™ confectionery coating daisies, using the color contrast method on page 34. Tint coconut. Mix two teaspoons milk and a few drops of food color in a plastic bag. Add coconut, twist bag to seal, then knead until evenly tinted. Spread on paper towels to dry. Pipe a few tube 225 drop flowers.

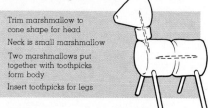

Trim marshmallow to cone shape for head

Neck is small marshmallow

Two marshmallows put together with toothpicks form body

Insert toothpicks for legs

2. Make the little lambs as diagram shows. Brush thinned royal icing over entire lamb. Pipe ears with tube 3. Cover legs, neck, ears and head with tight curls piped with tube 1. Brush additional thinned icing on body, and press on white coconut. Pipe tail and hooves with tube 3, features with tube 2. Attach drop flowers with icing for "necklaces".

3. Bake, fill and ice an 8″ two-layer square cake. Pipe a tube 6 bulb border at base, tube 4 at top edge. Drop guidelines, then pipe tube 19 zigzag garlands. Add stars at points. Attach daisies with icing. Place a 6″ round cake circle on cake top, then edge with tube 6 bulbs. Let icing set, then cover circle with tinted coconut. Set the little lambs on their grassy patch and serve to twelve.

The name eggs, at right are filled with delectable marshmallow or chocolate cream, then dipped in pastel Candy Melts™ confectionery coating or luxurious chocolate. Here's how to make them.

Double chocolate eggs

A truly deluxe treat that will thrill every chocolate lover! Here's the easy way to make the rich fudgy centers.

Chocolate cream fondant*

  1⅓ cups hot water
  4 cups granulated cane sugar
  ½ cup light corn syrup
  3 ounces unsweetened chocolate, chopped
  2 tablespoons butter

Before you begin, melt chocolate over hot water, stirring constantly.

The best way to work fondant is on a marble slab, using metal candy bars, arranged on it in a 12″ x 18″ rectangle to contain it. If these are unavailable, use a heavy 12″ x 18″ cookie sheet with 1″ sides. Have a paint scraper at hand. If your stove is electric, turn heat unit to highest temperature.

1. Stir hot water, sugar and corn syrup together in a three-quart heavy saucepan. Place over high heat and stir constantly until all sugar crystals are dissolved. Wash down sides of pan with a pastry brush dipped in hot water. Clip on thermometer and continue cooking without stirring, to 240°F, washing down sides of pan twice more as mixture cooks. Remove from heat. Entire cooking process takes about twelve minutes.

2. As soon as bubbles subside, pour mixture onto marble slab, or cookie sheet. Allow to cool, undisturbed, until fondant holds the imprint of your finger and feels lukewarm, about eight minutes. Cut butter in small pieces and scatter over surface. Pour melted chocolate over fondant. Remove metal candy bars.

Please turn the page

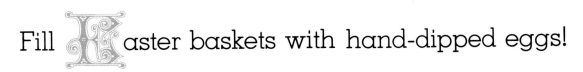

59

A candy box Egg . . . an Easter masterpiece

Mold this magnificent box in the Egg pan set, trim it with fanciful curves and cut-outs, then fill it with molded chocolates. A sensation!

1. Mold the box in Candy Melts™ confectionery coating. Use this procedure for a large box with thick, even walls. For each half of the egg, melt two pounds of coating. Spoon melted coating around inside edge of pans, allowing it to run down to bottom. Place pans on cookie sheet, supporting on ring or crumpled foil. Refrigerate for about 10 minutes for a hardened shell. Repeat four or five times until walls of box are ½" thick. Unmold on paper towels.

2. Flatten the bottom of the box by setting it on a cookie sheet placed over a pan of hot tap water. The coating will melt slightly to form a flat bottom. Set on wax paper to harden.

3. Trim the box. To avoid finger prints, wear thin knit cotton "cosmetic" gloves. For lower border of lid, turn upside down. Mark the edge with a pin at ½" intervals. Stretch ½" ribbon across lid and mark where ribbon will be fastened. Now fill a paper cone fitted with tube 1s no more than ⅓ full of melted coating. Connect the marks with scallops, omitting spaces for ribbon, then add dots and fleurs-de-lis. Turn lid right side up.

To guide upper row of scallops, mark with the lid of the largest mold of the Egg mold set. Divide into even spaces, mark with a pin and drop strings from mark to mark, omitting spaces for ribbon. Add dots. Finish with contrasting dots and flower cut-outs (page 47) made with a truffle cutter. Pipe scallops and dots around edge of lower part of box.

4. Stretch ½" ribbon across lid allowing about 6" extra length. Attach ends to inside of lid with melted coating. Form a loop near one end of a 9" ribbon. Fasten to inside of lid with plenty of melted coating, allowing loop to extend as handle. Repeat on other side. Add a fluffy bow.

5. Make base for box of double corrugated cardboard, using pan as pattern. Cover with foil and border with a ruffle. Stroke melted coating on base and set box on it. Fill the box with candies molded from real chocolate, and wrapped in thin foil. Fabulous!

Name eggs, con'd

3. Now work the fondant with a scraper, lifting it up from all sides and keeping the mass in constant motion. When the fondant is stiff enough to hold the scraper straight up, it is finished. Knead briefly and place the ball of fondant in a container. Cover with a damp cloth, then cover the container. Use at once or refrigerate for up to three weeks. Yield: 40 eggs or 200 centers.

1. **To mold the eggs,** knead the fondant briefly. Spray Large egg mold sheets with non-stick pan release. Break off pieces of fondant and push into the mold depressions, filling level and smoothing off excess with a spatula. Refrigerate until firm. Use a spatula to lift one edge of egg, then invert mold to drop out egg. Press two halves together.

2. Before dipping in chocolate, you must first temper the chocolate. This is a very easy process if you have your most important tool at hand—a low temperature thermometer. Read just how to do it on page 143.

3. Dip the eggs. You'll find dipping centers in real chocolate even easier than dipping in confectionery coating. The consistency of the chocolate makes it cling readily to the centers. Set up your work area and dip exactly as described on page 42.

Trim the eggs by piping names with tube 1 and royal icing thinned with piping gel. Attach made-ahead drop flowers with dots of icing.

Dainty pastel eggs
For the marshmallow centers, use the recipe on page 144 or your own.

1. To mold the eggs, spray Large egg mold sheets with non-stick pan release, then dust with cornstarch. Fill prepared molds with a teaspoon. Do not overfill. Allow to firm overnight at room temperature.

2. To unmold the eggs, lift one edge gently with the tip of a small spatula, then invert into a cookie sheet filled with a mixture of ¼ cup cornstarch, ¼ cup confectioners' sugar. Put two half-eggs together by brushing flat surface of one with water, then placing second half-egg on it.

3. To dip the eggs in confectionery coating, follow the method on page 42. Melt about 1½ pounds of coating. For a very smooth surface, dip a second time.

Fabulous Easter baskets

Fill their baskets with candy eggs, each with a cute little pet seated inside. Watch their eyes shine!

1. Mold the eggs with Candy Melts™ confectionery coating and lower halves from the Egg mold set. For hollow eggs, use the method for Valentine box, page 143. The pink and yellow eggs are molded in the largest egg mold, the white egg in the medium size mold.

2. Trim the eggs. Edge pink egg with royal icing drop flowers attached with dots of melted coating. Decorate yellow egg with melted coating in a parchment cone. Use tube 2 for strings and dots, tube 501 for shells. Use melted coating and tube 2 for trim on white egg.

3. Mold the bunny and lamb in plastic molds using the color contrast method on page 34. Figure pipe the chicks with Figure piping icing on wax paper. Build up round body with tube 1A. Insert tube 12 into body and pipe head. Use tube 10 to pull out wings and tail. Pipe eyes with tube 3, add tube 65s beak.

Easter bunnies made of marshmallow!

Use the marshmallow recipe on page 144, firming it in two 8″ square pans for a ½″ depth. Turn out onto a cookie sheet filled with tinted crystal sugar. Cut out bunnies with a cookie cutter dipped in cold water. Sprinkle with more sugar. Use tube 1 and piping gel for features and attach a jelly bean to each with a dot of royal icing.

Panorama eggs are Easter treasures! Figure pipe chirping chicks and chubby bunnies to perch inside. The eggs are molded of sugar—special sparkle comes from glitter stirred into the sugar!

Chicks in a blue egg

1. Use the medium size egg from the Egg mold set. Mix three cups of sugar with liquid food coloring, about two teaspoons of glitter and enough egg white so mixture is just evenly damp. Pack into halves of mold and turn out on cardboard. Flatten base of egg with a taut thread. With a toothpick, outline flat oval area on one half of mold. Let dry about an hour, then carefully pick up and spoon out damp sugar leaving a ¼" thick shell. Mold solid base in the bottom half of the small egg mold. Dry. Pipe royal icing drop flowers with tubes 225 and 106.

2. Figure pipe body and head of chick with Figure piping icing and tube 12. Add beaks and eyes with tube 1, wings with tube 5. Dry.

3. Assemble egg with royal icing. Pipe a mound of icing on base and set rear half of egg on it. Attach flowers to rear wall of egg, then secure chicks. Pipe a little tube 233 grass on either side. Cut out marked opening in front half of egg with a sharp knife. Run a line of icing around edge of rear half of egg and gently press front to it. Add a few more flowers and grass to interior. Pipe a tube 102 ruffle around seam, tube 1 beading around opening and base, tube 1s piping gel scallops. Add a ribbon bow.

Pink egg with bunnies

1. Mold and assemble the egg just as for the blue egg. You will need four cups of sugar, plus three teaspoons of glitter. Use the largest egg mold.

2. Figure pipe the bunnies. Holding tube 12 straight up, pipe pear-shaped body, then head. Use tube 5 to pipe legs, ears and puffy cheeks. Dry, then do features and inside of ears with tube 1s and piping gel. Give each bunny a jelly bean to hold and a jaunty bow.

3. Pipe tube 1 bulbs at seam, opening and base. Polka dot egg with piping gel and tube 1, then trim with drop flowers, tube 65 leaves and ribbon bows.

Quick & Pretty

Pastel petits fours eggs

Make these dainty treats in a hurry, then present them on a silver tray for a beautiful Easter treat.

Bake the cakes in Egg minicake pans and ice with buttercream. Cover with Quick poured fondant, either chocolate or tinted in pale pastels. Decorate with small drop flowers (perhaps saved from another project), tube 1 stems and designs, tube 65 leaves.

H is for new <u>Flowers</u>, piped or newly-made of candy! For <u>Figures</u> made of candy, too. And for <u>Father's day</u> and <u>First Communion</u> cakes.

Pure white lilies trim a cake for First Communion

1. Make the royal icing lilies first, then decorating the cake is a breeze! Use a 1⅝" two-piece lily nail and tube 75. Pipe six pointed petals, starting deep within the nail, then center with a green tube 16 star. Dip tips of seven artificial stamens in thinned yellow icing, dry and push into the star.

2. Bake a cake in the cross pan and ice smoothly with buttercream. Set on rack over cookie sheet and cover with poured fondant. One recipe will cover the cake. Place on serving tray. Pipe message with tube 1. Do the petal border with tube 4. Pipe two horizontal bulbs, then center with an upright bulb and a dot. Continue around cake.

Arrange lilies on mounds of icing and trim with tapering tube 68 leaves. Serve to twelve. The lilies are souvenirs of the occasion.

Sunny daffodils brighten an engagement cake

The flowers are made of candy, and are entirely edible! Turn the page to see how they're made. The cake itself is simply decorated to set off the showy new flowers.

1. Bake a two-layer 12" round cake and a single-layer oval tier. Ice with buttercream and assemble on tray. Set oval tier to rear of round tier. Divide 12" tier into sixteenths and mark midway on side.

2. Pipe tube 16 base and top shell borders on both tiers. Write message with tube 1. Pipe a tube 14 zigzag garland from mark to mark on base tier, then cover with tube 124 swags. Add tube 16 fleurs-de-lis and tube 14 stars at points. On tier top, pipe a tube 124 curve, then jiggle your hand twice before piping next curve. Edge top of oval tier with a tube 104 pleated ruffle. Now arrange the sprays of candy daffodils. Serve this springtime beauty to 28.

Use this recipe for the new flowers. Directions for making them are on page 68.

Candy for flowers

    4½ ounces Candy Melts™ confectionery coating (by weight)
2 drops Candy flavoring
Candy color
2 ounces glucose (by weight)

1. Melt the coating (page 42). Stir in flavoring and coloring, drop by drop. Heat the glucose until just warm and stir into melted coating. Mixture will appear curdled. Scrape out onto plastic wrap, wrap tightly and refrigerate one hour (or up to three weeks).

2. Remove from refrigerator. Mixture will be rock-hard. Break off a piece about 1½" square and knead with your fingers until smooth and pliable. Continue kneading portions, then combine into one mass. The candy will be smooth and somewhat greasy. Makes 8 tulips or 100 wild roses.

Brand new beautiful  Flowers...

Here's an exciting, and very easy, *new* way to fashion beautiful flowers to trim your cakes. It's quick and it's fun. First make the recipe on page 67.

1. All the flowers shown here were formed with cutters from the Flower garden set. Use the tools that come with the set, too.

2. Roll out on a clean smooth surface. Roll to ⅛" thickness for all petals and for tulip and daffodil leaves. Roll other leaves thin as possible. Cut and assemble the flowers. Attach one part to another by pressing. The candy mixture is very pliable, so the flowers are easy to form. There's no waste—knead scraps back into the mixture. Store, tightly wrapped in plastic, for weeks. Needs no refrigeration. Knead to use again.

3. Harden all flowers and leaves overnight or longer. Leave them in the foil, cups or formers to harden.

Daffodil. Cut two sets of petals with the daffodil petal cutter. Cover nail number 8 with foil. Lay one petal section in it, then gently press second section to first. Cut cup with daffodil cup cutter. Form over round end of stick 2, overlapping ends. Press edges with your fingers to ruffle and thin. Place on petals and press gently with stick. Use royal icing to pipe a tube 13 star, then three tube 2 stamens.

Tulip. Cut a petal section with small tulip cutter and one with large tulip cutter. Cut an egg carton into individual cups and cover cups with foil squares. Lay large petal section in cup, shape with stick 2, then add small petal section. Press with stick to attach, shape petal edges with fingers. Cover an artificial stamen with thinned green royal icing. Pipe black tips on six stamens. Dry. Pipe a tube 16 yellow star in center of tulip, bunch stamens and push into star. Remove stamens

fashioned from candy and delicious!

before serving.

Stems and leaves for tulips and daffodils. For stems, form a small cylinder of candy and roll it on surface to a long string. For tulip leaves, cut with the tulip leaf cutter, curve edges with fingers, harden within curved former. For daffodil leaves, cut with the lily leaf cutter. Cut each leaf into five strips. Harden in curved former.

Rose. Cut five petals with the small rose leaf cutter and twelve with the large leaf cutter for a full-blown rose. Cut a calyx for each flower with calyx cutter. Model a cone about ¾" high from candy. Thin edge of a small petal with your fingers, and wrap around the top of cone. Wrap a second small petal, point down, tightly around first. Add three more small petals, furling and thinning edges with your fingers. Now add large petals, pressing points against cone to attach. Thin and furl each petal as you attach it. Curl points of calyx and press to bottom of rose. For bud, wrap five small petals around cone, but do not furl edges. Press on calyx.

Wild rose. An easy, one-piece flower. Cut flower with the briar rose cutter. Place on palm and curl petals by pressing with round end of stick from edge to center. Harden within curved form. Cut leaves with small rose leaf cutter and calyx. Curl points of calyx with your finger and press to back of flower. Add royal icing tube 000 stamens. Press leaves in leaf vein mold and harden in former. For bud, fold a flower shape in two, wrap around a ½" pointed cylinder of candy and shape with fingers. Add calyx.

See cakes trimmed with these new flowers on pages 67, 99, 127 and 141.

Would you believe this darling little First Communion doll is made of Candy Melts™ confectionery coating and wears a candy dress? The process is quick and easy.

Use the ten-year-old mold from the People Mold set. Work in as cool a room as possible so the heat of your hands will not melt the small pieces of molded coating. All seams are easily smoothed by rubbing with a damp Handi wipe.

Molding the figure

1. Very lightly rub all molds with vegetable oil. For lower body, fasten two parts of mold together with a rubber band. Spoon a few drops of melted coating on bottom of mold (feet openings) and cover with a square of wax paper. Drop a little coating on the paper and set the mold on a piece of 1" styrofoam. Let coating harden. Bend a piece of stiff florists' wire into a hairpin, 4½" long. Push hairpin through mold and wax paper into styrofoam, making sure wire does not touch sides of mold.

Melt 6 ounces of white coating (page 42) adding pink and yellow Candy color as you stir. Pour into mold, still on styrofoam, one teaspoon at a time, tapping frequently to work out air bubbles. Place in freezer for 10 to 15 minutes. (You will know coating

has hardened by the crackling sound it makes as warm air hits the mold.) Release molded figure.

2. For head and upper body, secure mold halves with rubber band, then fill by teaspoon, tapping frequently. Insert a toothpick into the filled mold to support neck and head. Put in freezer for 10 to 15 minutes. Lift mold off front of figure carefully so as not to damage the face. Remove lower part of mold. (Toothpick makes this easy.)

3. For the arms, fill cavities on each half of mold. Hold halves over pan of coating and quickly place together. Press to squeeze out excess coating, secure mold with rubber band and place in freezer 8 to 10 minutes. Unmold.

4. Adjusting the arms. To bend the elbows, you must first cut through the arms. Cut out a wedge at the elbow with an artist's knife, about ⅛" wide at inner part of arm, ⅜" wide at outer part. Dip cut ends in melted coating and press together. Set upper body on a piece of styrofoam and hold arm to it to judge position. Adjust while coating is still wet. Make sure elbows are close to body. Harden arms on wax paper. Smooth joints and seams with a damp handi wipe. Handle as little as possible

to prevent softening. Smooth seams on all pieces.

5. Apply makeup with powdered chalk, just as described in the booklet that comes with the molds. Do this while head and upper body is on a styrofoam block, secured with end of toothpick. Hold the block, not the molded piece. If you make a mistake, rub off, with handi wipe, apply again.

Dressing the figure

1. Assemble upper and lower figure. Push wires on feet into a block of styrofoam. Clip off loop of wire on top to ¼" length. Clip off end of toothpick on upper body. Dip upper body into melted coating, press to lower body, let harden and smooth.

2. All clothing is made from the Candy for Flowers recipe on page 67 omitting color and flavoring. Use white confectionery coating. As you knead the mixture, work in drops of White-White liquid icing color to lighten. Roll paper-thin.

3. For socks, cut a strip ¾" x 2". Starting at toe, rub strip as you wrap around ankle, seam at back. Rub to smooth. If socks are not level, push high spots down with edge of knife. For shoe, wrap a ¼" x 1" strip around foot, starting at toe. Trim excess at back and rub smooth. Cut out curve at top with

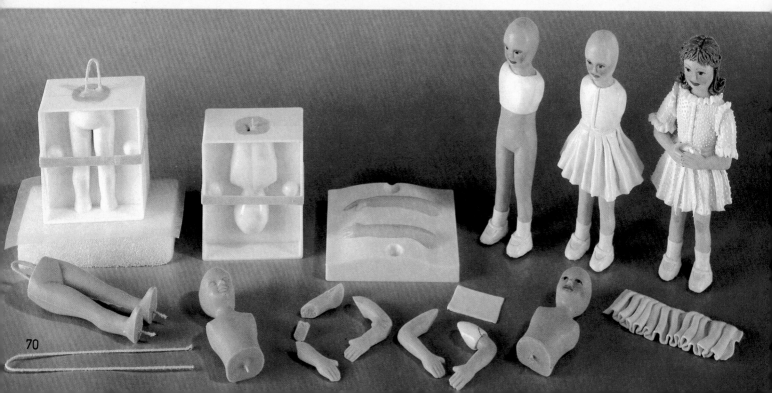

The sweetest 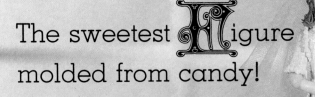igure molded from candy!

For directions for cake, please turn the page

knife. Rub on a tiny strip for strap, starting at inside.

4. For sleeve, cut a rectangle 1" x 1¼". Holding arm in a damp handi wipe, smooth strip around upper arm, seam on inside. Work sleeve over the top edge of arm, covering the edge of area where it will join shoulder. Rub to attach.

5. For bodice, cut a 1¼" x 3" strip and wrap around body, meeting in back. Rub to attach, trim excess and rub to smooth seam. Note armholes are covered. Carefully trim neckline with knife and rub smooth. Cut a ⅛" x 1¼" strip and rub to attach to bodice.

6. For skirt, cut a 1¾" x 8" strip. Roll one long edge with a stick to thin it. On this edge, make tiny pleats, using stick 4 to adjust folds. Pleated strip will measure about 3" long. Lightly rub top of pleats. Clip a crumpled strip of plastic wrap around upper legs to support skirt. Carefully lift pleated skirt, wrap around body just touching bottom of bodice, and roll with stick 4 to attach. Adjust pleats by lifting with a stick. Trim skirt to even length.

Finish the figure

1. Run a ⅛" ribbon around waist. Attach bow with royal icing.

2. With royal icing, pipe a tube 101s ruffle around arm at top and press to shoulder. Do the same for other arm and quickly adjust positions so one hand lies on top of the other. Hold until set. Dry.

3. Polka dot the dress with tube 000 and royal icing. Add neck and sleeve ruffle with tube 101s, buttons for bodice and shoes with tube 1s. Pipe hair with tube 1. Pipe drop flowers with tube 13. For veil, cut a 10" circle of tulle. Fold in half and mark a 2" space in center of folded edge. Gather this space to 1", then attach to head with royal icing. Secure wreath of flowers.

A pretty new lower with a funny name

The alstroemeria blooms in fluffy clusters of pink and gold. Everyone loves them—especially brides. Duplicate this flower in icing, then use it to trim a sensational cake for a wedding announcement or shower. Alstroemerias look just as pretty on a wedding or birthday cake.

The centerpiece cake

1. Pipe about 90 alstroemerias in royal icing. Set aside to dry.

2. Bake, fill and ice a two-layer 12″ petal cake. Mark a 3″ circle in center of cake top. Pipe names with tube 1, then edge the circle with tube 2 dots and fleurs-de-lis. Make a mark 1″ up from base at each indentation on cake.

3. Pipe bottom and top shell borders with tube 16. Pipe a tube 88 zigzag garland on each curve of cake, from mark to mark. Add tube 14 fleurs-de-lis and stars at points. Cluster alstroemerias on each curve of cake top, setting on mounds of icing. Trim with slender tube 349 leaves. Add flowers to base of cake. Serve this showpiece to 26 guests.

Pipe alstroemeria in royal icing on a 1¼″ two-piece lily nail.

1. Pipe four tube 102 pink petals, touching at base.

2. Smooth center with a damp artist's brush.

3. Add two tube 349 upright yellow petals. Let set, then pipe tube 1s brown dots.

4. Pipe a pink tube 14 star in base. Insert artificial stamens. Tube 1 covers stamen tips and pipes green points on petals.

The First Communion cake
shown on page 71

1. Cut a 4″ circle from 1″ thick styrofoam for platform for figure. Ice with royal icing. Pipe daisies with tubes 101, 102 and 104. Add piping gel centers with tube 3. Dry within curved form.

2. Bake a 10″ round layer and a layer in the 10″ top bevel pan. Fill and ice smoothly with buttercream. Cover with rolled fondant. Divide cake top into twelfths and mark at top edge of bevel. Connect each mark with mark directly opposite to form radiating design. Make marks on lower edge of bevel halfway between upper marks.

3. Pipe a tube 4 bulb border at base of cake. Outline radiating design with tube 2, then drop strings to form scallops. Let icing set, then fill in every other space with yellow piping gel, applied dot-fashion with tube 3. Cover all outlines with tube 2 beading. Drop tube 2 triple parallel strings on side of cake, starting with marks on lower bevel edge. Trim points with dots. Attach platform to cake top with icing. Secure figure to platform by pushing in wires on feet. Trim platform and cake with daisies, then pipe tube 67 leaves. Serve this radiant cake to 14.

Dad doesn't always get all the attention he deserves—so set aside this day to let him know how special he is. Bring him breakfast in bed with the Sunday paper, serve his favorite foods for dinner. Then surprise him with a cake baked just for him!

King of his castle

Express your appreciation with this royal crown made of cake and icing and completely delicious.

1. Bake and fill a two-layer 12" hexagon cake, a single-layer 8" round cake and a half-ball cake baked in the Ball pan. Ice hexagon and round cakes and assemble with half-ball cake on cake board. Divide and mark half-ball into quarters. Divide round cake into twelfths and mark midway on side.

2. At each corner of hexagon, pull up a tube 199 upright shell. Fill in base border with tube 18 rosettes. Pipe message with tube 3. Pipe stars on corners and at top edge with tube 18. Pipe a tube 5 bottom and top bulb border on round cake. At each mark, pipe a tube 12 ball and flatten for "jewel". Edge with tube 3 beading.

3. On half-ball cake, pipe tube 2B lines at divisions. Fill rest of area with tube 16 stars. Now add a circle of tube 172 upright shells. Pipe another at top of crown and finish with tube 5 balls. Fit for royalty! Serve to 31.

A medal of honor

The medal and its ribbon are quickly made from rolled-out stiffened buttercream.

1. Make two recipes of Snow-white buttercream, page 83. Take out five cups from the batch to make medal. Blend in 1¼" cups of confectioners' sugar to stiffen.

heart on Hather's day

Leave one cup of this mixture untinted. Divide remainder in half—tint one half red, the other gold. Tape wax paper to the back of a cookie sheet. Place gold icing on it, cover with wax paper and roll out to ¼" thickness. Do the same for red and white icings, but roll out to ⅛" thickness. Place in freezer for an hour or more. Remaining Snow-white buttercream will be used to ice and decorate the cake.

2. Bake, fill and ice a two-layer 9" x 13" sheet cake. Remove cookie sheets from freezer and peel off top layer of wax paper. Using *Celebrate!* pattern, cut out bar, cross and ribbon stripes with an artist's knife. Assemble on cake top, starting with bar. Use a miniature cutter to cut out red hearts. Do lettering, beading and fleurs-de-lis trim with tube 2.

3. Pipe tube 199 upright shells all around base of cake. Add double interlaced strings and dots with tube 3. Pipe a top shell border with tube 364. Attach hearts with dots of icing and pipe a tiny tube 2 heart in center of each. Dad will love it! Serve to 24.

 is for <u>Graduation</u>. Celebrate this <u>Grand</u> event with a cake that salutes their <u>Glorious</u> achievement!

Good luck, grads!

What better symbol of the graduates' superior mental ability than the wise old owl?

1. Make the book. A piece of cake, 5½" x 4½" forms the pages. Ice sides with tube 1D and buttercream. Cut the binding from tinted rolled fondant. Cut a 1" x 6" strip for backbone and press to long side of cake. Cut two 6" x 5" pieces for front and back and allow to dry flat. Attach to book with icing.

2. Make the owls on wax paper. For each you will need two half-eggs baked in the Egg minicake pan. Ice flat sides together, then trim off base so egg will stand upright. Ice a marshmallow and attach to top of egg with a toothpick. Pipe two big eyes with tube 199 stars. Add tube 3 circles, flatten, then add tube 1 dots. Work from the bottom up to pipe tube 101 feathers. Pull out long strokes for wing feathers. As you near the head, change to tube 1 and pull out short lines. Pipe a tube 2 beak. From rolled fondant, cut two 1½" squares and two tube 1A buttons for hats. Dry flat. Make two tassels from gold cord.

3. Prepare the cake. Bake, fill and ice a 10" two-layer cake. Divide cake into twelfths and mark 1½" up on side. Set on serving tray and pipe a tube 17 bottom shell border. With tube 19, pipe double swags from mark to mark. Top with graduated tube 17 stars. Pipe a tube 19 zigzag border on top of cake. On backbone of book, pipe a tube 1 message.

4. Set book on cake top. Set owls on book on mounds of icing. Pipe claws with tube 3. Attach square hats, then tassels, then buttons. A pair of amazingly realistic owls! Serve cake to 14 guests.

Hooray!

An impressive tier cake that's easy to decorate and very expressive of the graduates' feelings.

1. Bake, fill and ice a two-layer 12" x 4" square tier and a two-layer 6" x 3" round tier. Assemble on cake board with 7½" legs from the Crystal-clear set and a 6" round plate. Divide 6" tier into twelfths and mark 1" below top edge. Mark a circle within each corner of top of base tier with a 3½" cutter.

2. On base tier, pipe "Hooray" with tube 14 on side. Pipe tube 20 bottom and top shell borders, then add a fleur-de-lis on each corner. With same tube, pipe curved shell and fleur-de-lis trim on top of tier, using circles as guides. Add fleurs-de-lis between circles.

3. On top tier, pipe tube 17 bottom and top borders. Pipe tube 16 fleurs-de-lis at marks, then use the same tube to drop strings and pipe stars at points. Crown with Glad graduate figure and serve to 42.

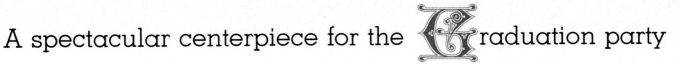
Make the day doubly special with this cake that symbolizes the arduous steps the graduate took to reach her goal! Carry out the school colors in the stairway carpet and flowers so the cake is truly individual.

You will need a Filigree stairway and bridge, a Glowing grad figure and a Flower spike.

Make trims in advance

1. Prepare the stairway. You will need a recipe of rolled fondant, page 85. Knead in color, then roll out as described on page 52. Use *Celebrate!* pattern to cut out the bridge carpet. Smooth the carpet over the bridge, trimming with a sharp knife at edges if necessary. Now cut out the stairway carpet, using pattern, and carefully fit it over the stairway. Trim at top and bottom as needed. Set aside to dry thoroughly.

Use oval pattern to cut out six ovals from fondant. Dry, then letter the graduate's subjects with tube ls. Dry again, then attach to risers of stairs with dots of royal icing.

2. Pipe the royal icing flowers. Do poppies with tube 102. Pipe a tube 5 dot in the center and push in a cluster of artificial stamens. Pipe daisies with tube 103 petals and tube 3 piping gel centers. Dry all flowers within curved forms. Prepare a bouquet for top of cake and two small clusters for bottom of stairway by mounting flowers on wire stems. Pipe tube 68 leaves on wires. Dry, then twist stems together to form clusters and bouquet.

3. Make the banners from satin ribbon in school colors. Cut into triangle shapes, then glue to lollipop sticks. Letter school name with tube ls and royal icing.

Prepare the cake

1. Bake a two-layer 11" x 15" x 4" tier and a two-layer 8" x 3" round tier. Make sure the heights of the tiers are accurate so the stairway will fit properly. Fill and ice both tiers. Set bridge on round tier, ½" from edge. Ask a friend to help you determine position of round tier. Hold round tier above and slightly to one side of base tier as your friend holds the stairway. Position round tier and remove stairway.

2. Divide round tier into tenths and mark at top edge. Divide short sides of base tier into thirds and mark at top edge. Mark long sides of tier 4" in from each corner. Repeat marks at base of tier. Mark curves at opposite corners of base tier for message.

Decorate the cake

1. On round tier, pipe a tube 16 base shell border. Drop double tube 3 strings from mark to mark, then add tube 16 upright shells and tube 14 stars. Pipe a tube 16 top shell border.

2. On base tier, pipe message with tube 2. Drop strings to guide columns from marks at top of tier to those at bottom. Pull up columns with tube 199. Drop double tube 3 strings from tops of columns. Add two curved shells and a star to top of each column with tube 199. Complete base border with tube 16 shells. Do top border with same tube.

Complete the picture

1. Arrange flowers on cake sides on mounds of icing. Trim with tube 68 leaves.

2. Set cake on party table. Attach stairway to bridge. Insert Flower spike just behind bridge. Fill with bouquet and banners. Wire clusters of flowers to bottom of stairway railing. Set graduate figure in position and stand back to admire! Serve to 45 graduates.

is for Halloween! Bake a Haunted House, or figure pipe a Horrible ghost to celebrate the holiday.

A 3-D haunted house

Send chills through the bones of the revelers with this upright haunted house. It's inhabited by ghosts, infested with spiders and alive with flying bats!

Do all the details first

1. Use indentations on pan as guides to cut out bats from black paper. For the lightning rod, dip a 4″ length of florists' wire in thinned black royal icing. When dry, pipe tube 5 black balls.

2. For the leafless tree, bend a dozen 12″ lengths of florists' wire in two. Bunch together and twist for trunk. Spread out branches and separate a few strands at bottom to make base. Paint with thinned black royal icing. The vulture's body is figure piped with tube 3 and black icing. Pipe head with tube 1. Attach to branch of tree with royal icing.

3. Windows, shutters and door are cut from Candy Melts™ confectionery coating. Melt, tint in lurid colors and spread the coating thinly on the backs of cookie sheets covered smoothly with foil. Spray backs of *Celebrate!* patterns with non-stick pan release and cut out. Let the coating just set up (about five minutes), then lay patterns on coating and cut around with a sharp knife. Let harden completely, then run a spatula under foil to release cut-outs.

Make the Haunted House

1. For this upstanding building, you will need two cakes baked in the Haunted house pan. For each cake, use six cups of pound cake mix batter. (Average box yields 3½ cups.) You will also need an 8″ single-layer square pound cake. Bake at 350°F for 40 minutes. Chill all cakes. Lay one house cake, top up, on surface. Ice top with buttercream and lay second house cake, top up, on it. Spread with icing and lay 8″ square on it, matching up bottoms. Trim bottom of cake level, insert a few toothpicks into layers, and stand upright on a foil-covered 12″ square cake board. Trim top of 8″ "addition" on a slant and fill crevices between house cakes with icing. Trim off one chimney section. An upright house, standing securely!

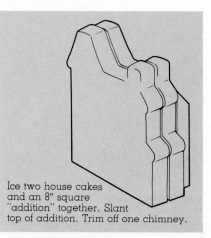

Ice two house cakes and an 8″ square "addition" together. Slant top of addition. Trim off one chimney.

2. Use buttercream for all decorating. Ice chimney smoothly and score for bricks. Starting at bottom, cover cake up to inverted "V" and lower roof with tube 15 stars. Pipe "V" and roof shingles with tube 104, allowing your hand to jiggle slightly for ramshackle effect. Continue piping stars up to roof line. Again, pipe the shingles with tube 104.

3. Press on the cut-out green windows. Pipe frames with tube 3. Now add the orange shutters on lines of icing. Let them hang in crooked positions. Attach left door half. Figure pipe the ghost with tube 1A, then add tube 3 hands and tube 1 features. Attach second half of door.

Complete the sinister scene

Pipe lots of spiders and spider webs with tube 0L. Push in lightning rod. Secure tree with icing to cake board. Use dots of icing to attach bats. This is a big building—the main house will serve 24 goblins. Cut the 8″ addition into six pieces.

A scary ghost

This menacing creature poses against a lurid Halloween moon and pallid candy stars. It's hard to imagine, but the cake was baked in the Noel pan!

1. Make the candy stars in advance, then decorating the cake will be a matter of minutes. Tape foil smoothly to the back of a cookie sheet—shiny side up. Melt about four ounces of Candy Melts™ confectionery coating and tint pale blue with Candy coloring. Spread the coating thinly over the foil with a spatula. Wait just a few minutes until it sets up but is not completely hardened. Use small cutters from the Star cookie cutter set to cut the stars. Place cookie sheet in the freezer for just a moment to harden completely. Take off tape and slide your hand under the foil. Stars will pop up. Save scraps to melt again.

2. Ice cake in chocolate buttercream. Following circular shape on cake, mark a crescent. Outline with tube 3, then fill in moon with tube 14 stars. Pipe bottom shell border with tube 16.

3. Simple low-relief figure piping forms the ghost. Use Figure piping icing or boiled icing thinned with a little corn syrup. With tube 1A pipe a long oval for head, pause, then increase pressure to pipe body, decreasing pressure and pulling down to side of cake. Insert tube into body and pull out arms. Change to tube 4 to pull out pointed fingers. Indent for features, then pipe eyes and mouth with piping gel and tube 3. Serve to twelve trick-or-treaters.

Invite a ghost to the Halloween party!

To cover cake, ice smoothly with buttercream and let icing crust. Place cake on cooling rack with a cookie sheet beneath it. Pour fondant over iced cake, flowing from center and moving out in a circular motion. Touch up sides with a spatula. Excess fondant can be stored, tightly covered, in refrigerator for weeks. Reheat to use again. Yield: 4 cups, enough to cover a 10″ round cake. Recipe may be doubled or tripled.

Chocolate poured fondant.

Follow recipe, page 84, but add 1 ounce of water. After heating, stir in 3 ounces of unsweetened, melted chocolate.

Wilton basic marzipan

Versatile and delicious! Make this easy recipe for modelled fruits, vegetables and figures , for rolled cut-outs or to make centers. Use it also for Australian and English method cakes.

    8 ounces almond paste
    2 egg whites, unbeaten
    ½ teaspoon vanilla or rum flavoring
    3½ cups sifted confectioners' sugar (approximate)

Crumble almond paste in a large mixing bowl. Add egg whites and flavoring and knead until thoroughly mixed. Now add the sugar, a cup at a time and knead very thoroughly after each addition until no lumps remain. Add enough sugar to the mixture so that marzipan has the texture of heavy pie dough. The entire process will take about 20 minutes.

Wrap closely in plastic wrap, then put in a tightly closed container and store for months in the refrigerator. When ready to use, bring to room temperature and knead again. If marzipan is too stiff, knead in a drop or two of warmed corn syrup until original consistency is restored. Yield: 1⅓ pounds or enough for about 38 fruits or about 100 centers.

Tint marzipan in two ways. Break off a portion and knead in liquid food color, a drop at a time. To tint brown, knead in cocoa. For tan, knead in dry instant coffee.

Or make a prepared tint. Put two teaspoons of kirsch or any white liqueur in a small container. Add liquid food color a drop at a time. Brush the color on the completed piece with a small artist's brush.

To roll out marzipan, dust work surface and your rolling pin with a sifting of confectioners' sugar. Roll out just like cookie or pie dough. Cut with gum paste or cookie cutters.

To attach pieces, dip or brush egg white on one piece and attach to second with a turning motion.

Always glaze completed fruits, figures or trims as soon as they have dried enough to hold their shapes. The glaze will keep them fresh and moist.

Corn syrup glaze

    ½ cup light corn syrup
    1 cup water

Combine syrup and water and heat to boiling in a small saucepan. Brush on marzipan pieces while hot. Allow pieces to dry at room temperature, 20 minutes.

Wilton rolled fondant

Give yourself a little time to practice and you'll find you can cover a cake with rolled fondant in just a few minutes. It gives a beautiful satin-smooth finish with softly rounded edges. Use only a firm pound cake or fruit cake.

    ½ ounce gelatin
    ¼ cup water
    2 pounds confectioners' sugar, sifted three times
    2 tablespoons solid white shortening
    ½ cup glucose
    ¾ ounce glycerine
    2 or 3 drops clear flavoring liquid food color, as desired.

Heat gelatin and water in a small pan until just dissolved. Put sifted sugar in a large bowl and make a depression in the center. Add shortening, glucose and glycerine to the dissolved gelatin and heat until shortening is just melted. Mix well. Pour mixture into depression in sugar and mix with your hands to a dough-like consistency.

Transfer to a smooth surface sprayed with nonstick pan release and lightly dusted with cornstarch. Knead until smooth and pliable. Add flavoring and color while kneading. If too soft, knead in a little confectioners' sugar. If too stiff, add drops of boiling water. Roll out as shown on page 52.

Use immediately or store in an airtight container at room temperature for up to a week. If storing longer, refrigerate and bring to room temperature before kneading and rolling out. Will cover a 14″ round or 12″ square cake. Recipe may be doubled.

Roll-out cookies

    1¼ cups butter
    2 cups sugar
    2 eggs
    5 cups all-purpose flour (approximate)
    1 teaspoon baking powder
    1 teaspoon salt
    ½ cup milk

Cream butter and sugar, add eggs and beat until fluffy. Sift dry ingredients together and add alternately to creamed mixture with milk. Turn out on lightly floured surface. Knead in more flour as necessary to make a firm dough. To tint, knead in paste food color applied with a toothpick. Refrigerate, wrapped tightly in plastic wrap, for an hour before rolling out.

Preheat oven to 325°F. Roll out on backs of lightly oiled cookie sheets to ⅛″ thickness with a lightly floured rolling pin. Bake about 12 minutes, checking frequently. Cool on wire racks. Wrap any unused dough tightly in plastic wrap and refrigerate for weeks. Bring to room temperature and knead to use again. Yield: 48 large cookies.

Please turn the page

Try these new icings and glazes for delicious results. Those made with real chocolate are luxuriously rich and designed to delight chocolate lovers. The pastel icing is daintily tinted and very smooth.

Chocolate glaze

1 pound semi-sweet chocolate, chopped
2 cups whipping cream
¼ teaspoon candy flavoring (optional)

1. Place whipping cream in pan and bring to a boil over medium heat. Remove from heat and add chocolate and flavoring. Stir until chocolate is completely melted. Refrigerate for one hour, or until mixture is the thickness of syrup.

2. This glaze may be poured over an uniced cake or one iced with buttercream. Place cake on rack over cookie sheet, then pour glaze slowly over it, touching up sides with a spatula if necessary. Allow glaze to firm 24 hours after pouring on cake. It will be shiny and very smooth. Recipe will cover a 10" round or square cake.

Chocolate ganache

1. Follow the recipe for Chocolate glaze through step 1. Refrigerate for one hour or more. Whip at high speed until fluffy. Let stand a few minutes until stiff. If mixture does not become fluffy after whipping, refrigerate again for about 20 minutes, then rewhip.

2. Use the Ganache for covering the cake and for roses, borders and stringwork. Handles easily and has a rich, smooth texture. Yield: about six cups.

Pastel candy cream

1 pound pastel Candy Melts™ confectionery coating
2 cups whipping cream
¼ teaspoon Candy flavoring

1. Combine coating and whipping cream in a heavy pan. Place over medium heat and stir constantly until mixtures comes to a boil. Remove from heat and stir in flavoring. Refrigerate overnight. Beat at high speed until peaks form.

2. Use for covering the cake only. Mixture will appear slightly separated, but will smooth out as you ice the cake. Very easy to handle. Too soft for borders or flowers. Yield: about six cups.

Stabilized whipped cream

A delicious covering for a cake! Use it also for simple borders. A cake with whipped cream trim should be stored in the refrigerator and served within two days.

1 teaspoon unflavored gelatin
4 teaspoons cold water
1 cup whipping cream
¼ cup confectioners' sugar
½ teaspoon clear vanilla extract

Combine gelatin and cold water in small saucepan. Let stand until thick. Place over low heat, stirring constantly until gelatin dissolves (about 3 minutes). Remove from heat and cool. Whip cream, sugar and vanilla until slightly thickened. While beating slowly, gradually add gelatin to whipped cream mixture. Whip at high speed until stiff. Yield: 2 cups.

Best-ever fruitcake

3 cups all-purpose flour
2 teaspoons baking soda
1 teaspoon baking powder
½ teaspoon cloves
½ teaspoon nutmeg
½ teaspoon cinnamon
½ teaspoon salt
1 pound candied cherries
½ pound mixed candied fruit
8-ounce jar candied pineapple
¾ cup dates
1 cup raisins
1½ cups chopped pecans (6-ounce package)
1½ cups chopped walnuts (6-ounce package)
½ cup butter
1 cup sugar
2 eggs
½ cup white grape juice
1½ cups applesauce (16-ounce can)

1. Preheat oven to 275°F. Sift and mix first seven ingredients. Cut up fruit and mix with nuts. Stir one cup of the sifted dry ingredients into fruit-nut mixture.

2. Cream butter and sugar. Add eggs and beat well. Beating until blended after each addition, alternately add remaining dry ingedients and grape juice to the creamed mixture. Mix in fruit-nut mixture and applesauce.

3. Turn into an 11" ring pan that has been sprayed with non-stick pan release. (Or use three 3½" x 7½" loaf pans.) Bake at 275°F for two and a half hours. Run a knife around sides of pan and let cake set ten minutes in pan. Remove cake and cool thoroughly.

Grandma's gingerbread

5 cups all-purpose flour (approximate)
1 teaspoon baking soda
1 teaspoon salt
2 teaspoons ginger
2 teaspoons cinnamon
1 teaspoon nutmeg
1 teaspoon cloves
1 cup vegetable shortening
1 cup sugar
1¼ cups unsulphured molasses
2 eggs, beaten

1. Thoroughly blend flour, soda, salt and spices. Melt shortening in large saucepan. Add sugar, molasses, and eggs; mix well. Cool, then add four cups of the dry mixture and mix well. Preheat oven to 350°F.

2. Turn mixture onto lightly floured surface. Knead in remaining dry ingredients by hand. Add a little more flour, if necessary to make a firm dough. Roll out on the backs of lightly oiled cookie sheets. Time baking according to thickness of rolled dough, from 7 to 14 minutes. Check frequently to avoid over-browning. Remove to wire racks. Cool about 30 minutes, then cover a flat surface with paper toweling and place baked pieces on it to dry overnight.

3. Wrap unused dough tightly in plastic wrap and refrigerate to keep for weeks. Bring to room temperature and knead briefly to use again. You will need two recipes for the castle, page 30.

 is for joyous 4th of July cakes trimmed in red, white and blue. Surprising just-for-fun cakes, too.

A double star for a patriotic picnic.
For directions, please turn the page.

Just-for-fun . . . make popcorn treats!

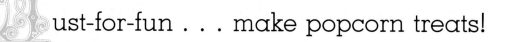

Surprise them with something really different! Pretty popcorn dessert cups, a pink popcorn panda—even a popcorn tier cake sweetened with candy!

Dessert cups add crunch, color and lots of class to ice cream. For 16 cups, just tint a half recipe of Holiday popcorn balls, page 34, and mold the cups over buttered bowls. Remove when cool, fill with a scoop of ice cream, top with whipped cream and a cherry.

A popcorn tier cake will really open their eyes! Mold the bottom tier in a 10" round pan, 3" deep and well buttered. Use 16 cups of popped corn and the syrup recipe for Holiday popcorn balls, page 34, increased by one fourth. Mix 1½ cups of small gum drops and

chocolate coated candies with the corn. Press firmly into pan.

Top tier is molded in a buttered 6" x 2" round pan. Use four cups of popped corn, ½ cup of candy and just a third of the Holiday popcorn ball syrup recipe, page 34. Assemble tiers with 5" clear pillars and 8" plates.

To dress up the cake, make gumdrop flowers. Cut gumdrops in half, flatten by rolling on granulated sugar and assemble by pressing petals together firmly. Leaves are made the same way. Dry for a few days before placing on "cake". To celebrate a birthday, add candles in Push-in holders.

Panda has extra tang. Mix six quarts of popped corn with this

recipe for syrup.
    9 tablespoons butter
    4½ cups miniature
        marshmallows
    12 tablespoons fruit-flavored
        red gelatin

Melt butter over low heat. Add marshmallows and stir until softened but not completely melted. Add gelatin and stir until mixture is evenly colored. (Gelatin does not need to be dissolved.) Pack firmly into buttered Panda pan. Unmold. We did the eyes and nose in the Color Flow technique right on the pan. Dry, then attach with corn syrup. Give him a little lollipop to hold.

Glaze all completed pieces with Corn syrup glaze, page 85.

A double star for a patriotic picnic *shown on page 87*

Pretty as a summer garden and perfect for a 4th of July picnic with its red, white and blue flowers.

1. Make the royal icing flowers in advance. Pipe the ruffly poppies with tube 102 on nail number 7. Add clusters of artificial stamens. Pipe tube 102 daisy petals on same nail, center with tube 4 flattened dots. Pull out petals for bachelor buttons with tube 13 on nail number 1. Centers are stars piped with same tube. Dry all flowers thoroughly.

2. Bake single-layer tiers—one in the Fancifill star pan and another in the 10½" star pan. Set each on its own cake board. Ice with

buttercream and assemble on serving tray with points of stars alternating. On top of upper tier, mark a line 1" in from edge.

3. Pipe tube 18 rosettes at base of lower tier. Pipe top star border with tube 17. Use the same tube for bottom and top borders on upper tier. Following mark, pipe contrasting tube 17 stars on tier top. Now arrange flowers on mounds of icing and trim with tube 67 leaves. Serve to 18.

Quick & Pretty
A spangled star

Just the cake for the picnic—showy lollipops double as decoration and treats for the children.

1. Make lollipops in plastic molds, and mold a few small stars, too. The recipe on page 34 takes only ten minutes. Make it twice—tint one batch blue, one red.

2. Bake and fill a two-layer 9″ star cake. Ice top smoothly and cover sides with tube 16 stars. Arrange an explosion of lollipops on top and attach a few small stars to sides. Serve to twelve.

Blast off!

Cake and candy combine to make a very realistic rocket.

1. Make eight fins from Candy Melts™ confectionery coating. Use the cut-out method, page 47 and *Celebrate!* patterns.

2. The base is a 10″ single-layer cake, the rocket itself is formed of five 6″ round layers, stacked and supported on 3″ clear pillars and 7″ clear plates.

Fill and ice the top of two 6″ layers, set on 6″ cake circle and insert a ring of four dowel rods. Ice top. Repeat with two more 6″ layers. Stack these two little layer cakes, then add the final 6″ layer. Ice sides and top—then place on separator plate. Push a long sharpened dowel rod through all layers down to plate and clip off level with top.

3. Ice 10″ base cake, insert a circle of six dowel rods and assemble with rocket with plate and pillars. Make cone with an 8″ circle of colored paper. Cut from center to edge, form into cone, tape and attach to rocket with icing. Edge base cake with tube 16 shells, rocket with tube 14 shells. Attach fins with icing. For the final touch, use boiled icing and tube 2A to make clouds of smoke. Serve to 22.

Just-for-fun, decorate these sweet cakes

Quick & Pretty

Enjoy!

Wrap a petite cake with a candy ribbon and present it to someone special—just-for-fun.

1. Bake, fill and ice a two-layer 6″ round cake. Write message on cake top with tube 2.

2. Double the Candy for Flowers recipe on page 67, using chocolate-flavored confectionery coating. Roll out to a long rectangle about ⅛″ thick. Using a ruler, trim off to 3½″ x 19″. Wrap around cake, folding neatly at seam. Ripple top edges by pressing with finger. Add a rose and bud (from your made-ahead supply) or any icing flowers. Trim with tube 70 leaves. Serves six.

Quick & Pretty

You're so special

A pretty cake says it much better than words!

1. Pipe royal icing drop flowers with tube 96. Add tube 2 centers and dry.

2. Bake, fill and ice a two-layer 9″ heart cake. Pipe tube 16 shell borders at base and top. Write tube 2 message. Now trim cake with tube 124 swags and attach flowers within curves. Add a tube 102 bow and a little flower cascade. Serves twelve.

is for cakes for the <u>Kindergarten</u> set. A little child takes such delight in a cake,

Little girls love dolls

Bake her a trio of pretty playmates and have a tea party! All the dolls have Egg minicake bodies, marshmallow heads, figure piped arms and legs and drop flower bouquets.

1. Pipe royal icing drop flowers with tubes 224 and 225. Dry. Bake cakes in Egg minicake pan, put halves together with buttercream and chill. Trim off bases of cakes so they stand securely. Thread a miniature marshmallow and a large marshmallow on a toothpick for head and neck. Dip in thinned icing tinted flesh color and stick in styrofoam to dry.

2. Ice the egg cakes, set on wax paper, then pipe arms and legs. For arms, use tube 12. Start with light pressure at shoulder and pull down to front of body, changing direction to give bend to elbow. (No hands are needed.)

For the blonde doll, first pipe balls for puff sleeves, then pipe arms. For legs, touch tube 2A to body and pull straight out. Use tube 12 to pipe ovals for shoes.

3. Use your imagination to dress the dolls in gaily colored clothing. Use tube 127 to pipe the red and pink skirts, tube 125 for the double-ruffled yellow skirt. Add beading with tube 2. Belts are

it's a pleasure to decorate it for him!

done with tube 46, collars and sleeve ruffles with tube 104 or 124.

4. Attach heads to bodies with toothpicks. Do eyes, cheeks and noses with tube 3, smiles with tube 1. Give each a hairdo with tube 1 or 13. Pipe a mound of icing at ends of arms and press in drop flowers. Trim with tube 65s leaves. Surprise a little girl!

Little boys love trains

Make him happy with this old-fashioned red Choo-choo, complete with bell, cowcatcher

and candy wheels.

1. Make the wheels, windows and head light from Candy Melts™ confectionery coating. Use the cut-out method, page 47. Cut four wheels with 2" round cookie cutter, two smaller wheels and head light with a 1½" round cutter. Cut 2 windows, 1⅝" x 1⅛", with an artists knife.

2. Bake a cake in the Choo-choo pan, using a pound cake recipe. Chill, then cut off bell from top of cake. Paint a 1" plastic bell with

thinned icing to replace it.

3. Attach windows with icing. Pipe cowcatcher with tube 16 lines. Do stripes around boiler with tube 46. Now cover the train with tube 16 stars. Press on wheels and head light. Pipe tube 46 drive-shafts to join wheels and add tube 16 rosettes. Attach bell with icing. Watch for that big wide smile! Serve to twelve young travelers.

The Kindergarten set loves flowers!

Little children are fascinated by flowers—growing in a pot, blossoming in a garden or blooming on a cake. Decorate one of these sweet daisy cakes for a sweet surprise. They'll love it!

Quick & Pretty

Daisy cupcakes

Bake a batch of cupcakes, swirl with icing and pipe tube 17 shell borders. Now hold the cake like a flower nail and pipe tube 127 petals. Center with a flattened tube 9 dot and sprinkle dot with sugar. Arrange on a tray in garden effect.

Quick & Pretty

A daisy tier cake

Watch their eyes light up when you bring in this flower-y tower-y tier cake!

1. Pipe royal icing "drop" daisies with tubes 1C and 2E. Center with tube 5 dots.

2. Bake and ice tiers, using one cake mix and Mini-tier pans. Assemble on tray with legs and plates from the set. Pipe tube 18 shell borders at base of all tiers, tube 16 borders at top. Now ring the tiers with daisies, attaching each on a mound of icing. Serve to twelve impressed children.

Cookie daisies bloom on a cake top

They'll eat the daisies, then enjoy the leafy cake.

1. Use a third-recipe of Roll-out cookies. Tint a small amount by kneading in cocoa. Divide remainder in half. Knead yellow food color into one portion and orange color into the other. Roll out and cut two sections for each flower with the daffodil petal from your Flower garden set. Cut centers with tube 2A. Lay popsicle sticks on baking sheet. Lightly press one petal section on end of stick, top with a second, then with a center. Watch carefully as daisies bake to avoid browning.

2. Bake, fill and ice a two-layer 8" round cake. Set on serving tray. Pipe bottom border with tube 70 and a shell motion. Pipe tube 112 leaves on top of cake in concentric circles, starting at outer edge. Plant daisies in cake and serve to ten flower lovers.

He's just irresistible! A cute little clown

1. Bake the cakes. For the clown you'll need a cake baked in the Petite doll pan for body and a cupcake for his head. The round base cake is an 8" single layer.

2. Ice the petite doll cake and set on the smaller plate of the Mini-tier set. (You'll be able to lift the clown off the base cake.) Thread two marshmallows together with a toothpick for each leg. Ice and attach to body. Figure pipe his arms with tube 2A, mitten-shaped hands with tube 7. Pipe ruffled cuffs with tube 101. Add a tube 125 neck ruffle and tube 5 buttons.

3. Now ice the top of the cupcake (this is the clown's face) and attach to body with a popsicle stick. Pipe eyes and nose with tube 5, smile with tube 3. Pull out spiky hair with tube 14 and do pompons on feet with the same tube. Attach a drop flower to a toothpick for the clown to hold.

4. Ice the base cake and set on serving tray. Do bottom border with tube 2B and a shell motion. Edge top with the same tube. Set clown, on plate, on top. Cut the base cake into five servings.

is for <u>Lace</u> . . . the <u>Loveliest</u> trim a cake can have. Here is a <u>Lesson</u> on how to pipe it.

Even a novice decorator can create a lace-trimmed masterpiece like this! If you can pipe a line, you can pipe lace.

There are many types of lace used in decorating, all adding a unique airy charm. The simplest lace is piped right on the cake. *Cornelli lace* fills an area with curved meandering lines, never touching. It is most effective when piped in white to veil a pastel ground. *Sotas*, borrowed from the Philippine style, is even quicker and easier. Even the familiar lattice is a form of lace.

Lace piped off the cake can be as delicately dramatic as these soaring butterflies or as precise as the tiny lace pieces often used on Australian cakes. You can curve lace, construct a little temple to crown a wedding cake with lace, even pipe dimensional forms in lace by using Australian nails, or by piping over a shaped form. Let the cakes on pages 51, 99, 147 and 154 inspire you—then add the magic of lace to your own masterpiece.

Tips on piping lace

1. Always use Egg white royal icing for strength. Don't overbeat the icing. This might lead to air bubbles. Thin the icing as needed with egg white so it flows easily from the tube.

2. Use a small parchment paper cone for best control. Keep an even, light pressure as you pipe.

3. Make sure that you join one line

of icing securely where it touches another line—otherwise the lace piece may collapse when you attach it to the cake.

4. Most important—*make extras*. If a lace piece is inadvertently broken, the extra lace you piped will give you peace of mind.

5. Attach lace pieces after cake is completely decorated. Always work from the top down.

Soaring lace butterflies . . .

enliven this ethereal petite wedding cake. Pipe the lace trims and flowers ahead of time, then put them on the simple cake.

1. Pipe the butterflies and lace side designs with tube 1 and Egg white royal icing on 10″ curved forms. Use *Celebrate!* patterns. You will need twelve butterflies and eight side designs, but make extras. The next page shows how to do it. Pipe wild roses with tubes 101, 102 and 103. Add tube 3 centers with yellow piping gel. Mount about 20 flowers on florists' wire stems. To make poufs, bunch a 4″ square of fine tulle in the center and secure with thin florists' wire. Twist stems of flowers and poufs together. Ice a 3″ half-ball of styrofoam to the plate of a small ornament base. Insert twisted stems for bouquet.

For ornament, glue a Card-

holding cherub to the plate of a small ornament base. Make a hoop of florists' wire and wire to hands. Cover with icing, then attach flowers with royal icing.

2. Bake and fill a 12″ x 2″ round layer and a 12″ top bevel layer for base tier. Top tier is a two-layer 6″ x 3″ round cake. Ice with buttercream, then cover with rolled fondant (page 52). Assemble with 7″ Crystal-look plates and 5″ pillars on a 13″ separator plate.

Accurate measuring is important. Divide top tier in fourths and mark top edge, corresponding to pillars below. On bottom tier, divide in eighths and mark on slanted bevel surface, again corresponding to position of pillars.

3. On base tier, pipe a tube 8 bottom ball border and trim with tube 1s scallops and dots. Attach lace flower designs to sides of tier with dots of royal icing, centering them between marks on bevel slant. Fill centers of lace flowers with piping gel and tube 1. Set bouquet within pilllars and adjust flowers. On top tier, run a tube 8 line of icing around bottom and attach flowers for border. Ice cherub ornament to top of tier and add more flowers to base.

4. On top tier, pipe a line of royal icing at each mark. Gently press a butterfly to icing, holding a moment until set. Attach butterflies to bottom tier the same way. Lower tier of this airy little masterpiece serves 68, top tier serves 16 guests.

There's lots of news in this lovely cake! Delicate lace pieces outline heart shaped trim, sotas softens the side curves, dainty flowers are formed from candy. The biggest surprise is the smooth glossy covering that sets off the whole design. It's candy, too!

1. Pipe about 120 lace pieces. Use Egg white royal icing, tube 1s and *Celebrate!* pattern. To make many lace pieces efficiently, trace the pattern many times in rows on paper. Tape this multiple pattern to a smooth surface (glass or plexiglass is ideal), then tape wax paper smoothly over it. Pipe the lace pieces, dry thoroughly, then run an artist's knife around edge of wax paper to loosen it. Slide the blade of a spatula under the wax paper to release the lace pieces.

2. Bake and fill a two-layer 10" square cake. Use a firm pound cake recipe. Chill, trim top level, then set on cake board and ice with buttercream. Let buttercream crust as you prepare candy.

3. Cover the cake. The recipe is the same as the Candy for Flowers recipe, page 67, but larger. Use 1 pound, 4 ounces of coating, 9 ounces of glucose and color and flavoring as desired. Knead the candy till smooth and pliable as recipe directs. Spray work surface with non-stick pan release, dust lightly with cornstarch. Roll out candy to an area large enough to cover entire cake, about ³/₁₆" thick. Drape over rolling pin and transfer to cake.

Now smooth the candy over the cake with your hands, starting at top center. The mixture remains so pliable you will have no trouble in smoothing it over the edges and corners. The excess icing at the corners can either be smoothed onto the sides of the cake or trimmed off and smoothed again. If a tear appears, simply patch with more candy and smooth. Trim off at base of cake, give a final smoothing and trim again.

4. Make the flowers. Use scraps of candy left over from covering the cake, but knead in more color. Cut with the violet cutter from the Flower garden set and follow the method for the wild rose shown on page 69. Omit calyx. Also cut a 1" x 4" strip from deeper-tinted candy. For leaves, make half of the Candy for Flowers recipe, page 67, tint green and cut with the small rose leaf cutter.

5. Decorate with either boiled or royal icing. Divide sides of cake into fifths and mark 1½" up from base. Drop string guidelines for curves. Press a 2¼" cutter to corners and a 3¾" cutter in top center of cake to define heart shapes. Place strip on top heart diagonally, press gently and trim.

6. Fill area from curves to base with sotas—curves and curls of icing piped randomly and sometimes overlapping. Use tube 1s. Outline curves, strip and all hearts with tube 1s bulbs. Pipe name with same tube. Pipe base bulb border with tube 5. Carefully secure flowers and leaves on dots of icing. Attach lace pieces by piping a small dot of royal icing on bottom of piece, then pressing very gently to outer edge of beaded heart. Start with the top heart and keep all lace at the same angle. This lacy showpiece will serve 20 party guests.

How to pipe *the lace designs shown on cake on page 97*

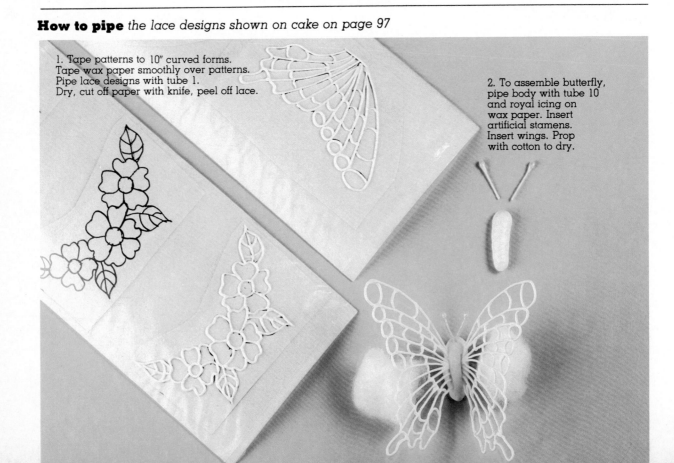

1. Tape patterns to 10" curved forms. Tape wax paper smoothly over patterns. Pipe lace designs with tube 1. Dry, cut off paper with knife, peel off lace.

2. To assemble butterfly, pipe body with tube 10 and royal icing on wax paper. Insert artificial stamens. Insert wings. Prop with cotton to dry.

A **L**ace-trimmed cake covered with candy

M is for cakes for your <u>Marvelous Mom</u> on <u>Mother's Day</u>. A flowery <u>May Day</u> cake, too.

Mother loves pretty things, so she'll be thrilled when you present her with a flouncy, flowery cake that spells out your love. Mold the letters and pink hearts in Candy Melts™ confectionery coating, then decorating the cake is easy.

A rosy loaf cake

1. Mold "Mother" and heart in confectionery coating. Pipe tube 225 drop flowers in royal icing and dry. Attach some flowers to letters with royal icing and trim with tube 65s leaves.

2. Bake, fill and ice a Long loaf cake. Divide short sides in half and mark midway on sides. Starting at corners of long sides, make three marks 1¾" apart, midway on sides. Drop string guidelines for ruffled garlands. Make an oval pattern 3½" wide and 3¼" deep and transfer to side of cake.

3. Run a tube 17 line around base of cake, then pipe pleated border with tube 104. Pipe ruffled garlands with same tube, then edge with tube 3 beading. Outline oval with tube 3 scallops. Pipe a tube 17 shell border at top of cake, then cover with a tube 104 pleated border. Attach heart within oval, edge with tube 3 beading and trim with flowers and tube 65s leaves. Add cluster of flowers and leaves to garlands. Finish the cake by setting the letters upright on mounds of icing on cake top. Support with toothpicks. Cut into 16 servings.

Love to Mother

1. Mold letters and hearts in confectionery coating. Use a Heart lollipop mold for the hearts. Pipe trim on letters with tube 1 and a mixture of half royal icing, half piping gel. Do script on hearts with tube 1s. Pipe royal icing wild roses with tubes 101 and 102.

2. Bake, fill and ice a two-layer 10" square cake. Pipe bottom and top shell borders with tube 16. Now do the scallops with the same tube. Pipe mounds of icing on corners of cake and arrange flowers in cascades. Trim with tube 65 leaves. Attach hearts to cake sides with icing and edge with tube 2 beading. Arrange letters on cake top, then present to Mother. Serves 20 guests.

Mom loves daisies

1. Mold letters and heart in confectionery coating. Trim letters with graduated dots piped with half piping gel, half royal icing and tube 1. Pipe royal icing daisies with tubes 102, 103 and 104.

2. Bake, fill and ice a two-layer 10" round cake. Divide side into eighths and mark 1½" above base. Make a mark at top edge midway between each mark below. Drop string guidelines for garlands.

3. Pipe zigzag garlands at base. Let set up then top with a second set of garlands on top of first for dimensional effect. Trim with tube 3 strings. Pipe garlands at top of cake the same way, then finish with a tube 17 rope border. Attach daisies within upper garlands and at base of cake. Pipe tube 67 leaves and arrange letters on cake top. This dainty creation serves 14.

Pink carnations for Mom

1. Mold a pink Candy Melts™ confectionery coating heart in the large Lollipop mold. Use a mixture of half royal icing, half piping gel to pipe scallops and dots with tube 2. Write message with tube 1s. Pipe ruffly carnations in royal icing with tube 104 on a tube 10 ball of icing.

2. Bake a cake in the Two-tier heart pan, ice smoothly with buttercream and cover with Quick poured fondant. Center candy heart on cake. Pipe a tube 9 bulb border at base of cake. Complete the decorating with scallops, dots

and beading piped with tube 2. Arrange the flowers on mounds of icing, then pipe slender tube 66 leaves. Serve to 12.

May baskets filled with violets

1. Make eight little May baskets from rolled fondant. Roll fondant about ⅛" thick, cut with *Celebrate!* pattern and lay over Tree formers covered with wax paper to dry for 24 hours. Pipe many tube 101 violets in royal icing with tube 1 centers. When dry, mount all violets on wire stems. Pipe violet leaves on wire stems with tube 69.

Make a few poufs 4" square from fine tulle, bunch in centers with fine wire. Combine flowers, leaves and poufs into eight bouquets by twisting stems together.

2. Bake, fill and ice a 12" x 4" two-layer petal cake. Pipe a tube 9 ball border at base, tube 7 border at top. Pipe a line of royal icing on long sides of a basket and press to side curve of cake. Repeat with remaining baskets. Attach a ribbon bow to each basket, then fill with bouquets. Remove baskets to serve to 26. The bouquets are the guests' souvenirs.

 is for <u>New Year's</u> celebration cakes and for cakes to present to your <u>Nice Neighbors</u>

Long life and prosperity!

That's the meaning of the oriental symbol on this showpiece cake. Symbol and lettering are done in Color Flow. This new-old technique gives a porcelain-like finish obtainable with no other method.

1. Do Color Flow pieces. The top ornament is done in two pieces for a dimensional effect. For red circle, tape *Celebrate!* pattern to a piece of plexiglass or stiff cardboard, tape wax paper smoothly over it. Outline with tube 2, then fill in with thinned icing, working quickly from outer edge in. Do the gold symbol the same way. Tape patterns for letters to 10″ curved forms. Tape wax paper smoothly over them, outline with tube 2, then fill in. Dry all pieces thoroughly, at least 48 hours. Define outlines on letters by piping again with tube 2.

2. Bake, fill and ice with buttercream a two-layer 10″ x 4″ round cake. Use a firm pound cake recipe. Cover with rolled fondant and set on serving tray.

3. Pipe a tube 6 ball border at base of cake and trim with tube 2 string. Attach letters to side with dots of royal icing. Now pipe and over-pipe riser lines on cake top to support circle. Use tube 4 and royal icing. Dry, then pipe dots of icing on lines and set circle in position. Attach gold symbol the same way. To serve to 14, run a knife under circle and lift off Color Flow pieces before serving.

The hour approaches!

1. The numbers, clock hands and letters are made of Candy Melts™ confectionery coating and the cutout method, page 47. Spread the coating about 1/16″ or more thick. Use Alphabet and Number cutters, a miniature cutter for the heart and *Celebrate!* patterns for the clock hands.

2. Bake, fill and ice a two-layer 14″ round cake. Pipe a tube 16 shell border at base. On top edge, pipe a line with tube 18. Pipe a second line just within it. Now top with a third line piped in the groove where the first two lines meet. Trim frame with tube 20 curved shells at four evenly spaced positions. Attach numbers to cake top, setting 1″ in from frame and using curved shell trim as guide. Pipe tube 14 shells to indicate hours, then a circle of tube 2 dots to indicate seconds. Finish by securing hands and letters with dots of royal icing. Serve to 36.

Use a pretty cake to tell your Neighbors

Quick & Pretty
Treats for two

Give a tray of pretty presents to the nice couple who walked the dog while you were away. They'll be thrilled—and will never guess how quickly you decorated them!

Just bake cakes in Little loaf pans. Ice with buttercream, then cover with poured fondant. When fondant has set, trim off edges neatly at base of cakes with a sharp knife. Tie up the cakes with tube 103 buttercream ribbons and bows and add a few drop flowers and tube 66 leaves. Each little cake makes two servings.

Welcome new neighbors

Give a get-acquainted party for the neighbors who just moved in to your block.

1. Pipe tube 131 drop flowers in royal icing. Dry. Bake a two-layer 10″ square cake and a cake in the Holiday house pan. Fill and ice the square cake with buttercream, top green, sides white. Divide sides into fourths and mark at base. Pipe trios of stems on sides with tube 2, then attach flowers and pipe tube 65 leaves. Pipe a tube 17 rosette bottom border, a tube 16 top shell border. Write greeting with tube 2.

2. Ice sides of house cake with yellow buttercream. Pipe tube 48 eaves, cover roof with tube 124. For shutters and door, pipe lines of buttercream with tube 48 on wax paper and put in freezer for about 30 minutes. Using pan as guide, outline windows with tube 2, then fill in with thinned boiled or royal icing. Pipe window frames with same tube. Using pan again as guide, trim off the frozen tube 48 lines and press to cake for shutters. Make door pattern and use to cut frozen lines. Press to cake. Pipe a tube 2 door knob.

3. Place house cake on square cake. Pipe tube 10 balls for bushes around house and cover with tube 349 leaves. Put on the coffee! Serve to 32 neighbors.

how nice they are!

Quick & Pretty
Bon voyage

See them off on their vacation with a goodby dessert party!

1. Bake a long loaf cake and ice with buttercream. Cover with poured fondant and place on cake board. Transfer *Celebrate!* pattern to cake top.

2. Divide long sides of cake into fourths and drop string guidelines for curves. Fill in from curves to base with tube 16 stars. Outline message on cake top with tube 3, let set, then fill in with tinted poured fondant and tube 2. Let harden, then finish by writing names with tube 1. Serve to 16 neighbors.

O is for Occupation . . . whether every-day work or spare time pleasure. Decorate a very personal cake to celebrate her hobby.

Nothing delights a person as much as a cake that celebrates his interests—the work he does for a livelihood or the hobby that gives him pleasure. Look through these pages for ideas, then decorate a special cake for your very special person. It will be perfect for many celebrations—a birthday, a retirement, or to say "Thank you" or "Congratulations" in a beautiful, personal way.

Dancing is her dearest occupation

Decorate a frilly, flowery cake and pose a little gum paste replica of her pretty self on top—dressed in a pink tutu and standing proudly in position one. She'll love it, and treasure the little figure for years.

1. Mold the figure in the 10-year-old mold of the People mold set. The next page shows how. Roll out gum paste to ⅛" thickness and cut plaque, using *Celebrate!* pattern. Hold figure above it to determine position, then make two holes for wires on feet. Dry.

2. Pipe royal icing sweet peas, varied tints of pink with tubes 102 and 103. Dry.

3. Bake a two-layer 9" x 13" cake. Fill and ice with buttercream and

place on cake board. Divide long sides into sevenths, short sides into fifths and mark 1" above bottom. Repeat the markings on top of cake, 1" in from edge.

4. Place gum paste plaque to rear of cake top. Attach a frame of sweet peas with dots of icing, then write message with tube 1. Pipe tube 16 shell borders at bottom and top of cake. Now drop tube 14 strings from mark to mark at base of cake. Repeat for double strings and add stars at points. Pipe matching scallops and strings on cake top. Pipe a diamond shape at each corner with tube 16 zigzags, extending down sides of cake. Press in sweet peas in a cascade, then pipe tube 66 leaves. To secure figure, flatten little balls of gum paste, dip in egg white, press to feet, then gently push wires on feet into holes on plaque. Present to a happy little girl and serve to 24 party guests.

Hail to the chef!
shown on page 111
Here he stands, triumphant, toqued and aproned, proudly presenting his specialty. If your man takes pride in his kitchen achievements, mold his replica in gum paste and set it on his favorite cake.

1. Mold the figure as shown on page 110, using the man mold from the People mold set. For the plaque, cut a 4" circle from gum paste rolled ⅛" thick. Hold figure

above it to determine position, then make holes for wires on feet.

2. Pipe 24 spoons with royal icing and tube 5. Handles are 1" long.

3. Bake and fill a 10" two-layer cake. Ice with mocha buttercream. Divide in eighths and mark midway on side. Lightly mark two concentric circles on cake top to guide lettering, 6" and 7" in diameter.

4. Edge plaque with tube 3 beading and print message with same tube. Decorate cake simply with Chocolate buttercream. Pipe a tube 16 bottom shell border. Drop double swags with tube 21 and do curved top shell border with same tube. Attach spoons with icing. To attach figure to plaque, flatten two tiny balls of gum paste, dip in egg white and apply to soles of shoes. Press wires on feet gently through holes in plaque into cake. Serve to 14.

Congratulations, Ellie

The People molds make it easy to turn out life-like little figurines with arms and legs in perfect proportion, and with the figures in proportion, one to another.

Use the recipe on page 36 and the general procedures described in the booklet that comes with the molds. Here we show you only the special methods that are unique to the figures pictured. You'll find lots of ways to make your own figures truly individual—in clothing, make-up and characteristic pose.

Use this updated method for rolling out gum paste for clothing. Brush a smooth work surface lightly with vegetable oil, then wipe off with a paper towel. Roll the gum paste on this surface (no cornstarch needed). The gum paste will be extremely thin and easy to handle and drape.

A cute little ballarina

If you've never molded in gum paste, start here. Mold legs and lower part of body in pink, head, upper part of body and arms in flesh-color gum paste. Make sure the feet are turned out in ballet position. Make up the face, then attach upper to lower part of body. Mold arms, hold to shoulders while wet to bend, then dry.

For bodice, cut a 1¼" x 3½" strip of thin gum paste. Brush egg white on dried figure, wrap strip around, meeting at back. Trim and smooth seam. Cut out for armholes. Cut ⅛" strips for shoulder straps and attach. For skirt, cut three 1" x 24" strips of fine tulle. Place together and gather one long side to measurement of waistline. For each shoulder ruffle, cut two tulle strips, ½" x 8". Slant ends, place together and gather to correct length. Attach both with royal icing. Attach arms and pipe hair with royal icing and tube 13.

The master chef

Use *Celebrate!* patterns for clothing. Dress figure in shoes, then shirt, then pants. Cut apron, attach to figure, then cut a 1½" x 1¾" thin piece of gum paste for towel. Paint stripes on edge with food color, pleat into folds, attach to apron. Cut a block of styrofoam for arm support. Hold arms to figure to judge how to trim support. Attach arms, let dry on support.

For food, cut oval tray with *Celebrate!* pattern. Model his specialty, then paint with food color. Attach to tray. (The flower basket and trowel are accessories for the figure on page 124.)

For chef's toque, cut a 2¾" circle of thin gum paste. Ice half a cotton ball to head, drape circle over it, paint a stripe of egg white around head, and pleat circle to it. Add a ⅛" strip for head band. Now pipe sideburns and hair with royal icing and tube 1. Attach tray to hands. Dinner is served!

Give your Mr. Fixit a big "thank you"

He keeps everything running smoothly. Show him how much you appreciate all he's done with a luscious chocolate cake!

1. Marzipan makes most of the trim. Tint a half-recipe of marzipan (page 85) in red, blue and brown, leaving other half untinted. Roll out about ⅛" thick. Use the 7" x 9" oval pan as pattern for the plaque, 2¾" and 1½" cutters from the Heart set to cut the hearts, and *Celebrate!* patterns for his tools. Set aside to harden, then brush

with Corn syrup glaze. Pipe messages on hearts with tube 1.

2. Bake, fill and ice his favorite two-layer cake. Use 9" x 13" pans and Chocolate buttercream or Chocolate ganache, pages 83 and 86, for filling and icing. Set on serving tray.

3. Tube 17 does all the decorating. Pipe rosettes for base border, curved shells for top border. Set plaque on cake, then edge with zigzags. Attach tools and hearts with dots of icing. Watch Mr. Fixit smile! Serve to 24.

Delight him with this 18-wheeler!

1. Start with the cookie trims. Using Roll-out cookie dough, page 85, and *Celebrate!* patterns, cut front and rear bumpers and windows. Cut headlights and hub caps with a 1" round cutter. Cut 18 wheels with 2" cutters. Bake and cool, then paint with thinned royal icing.

2. Prepare cake board and supports. Board is double corrugated cardboard, 25" x 7", covered with foil. Supports are

His ccupation: repairing everything that needs it!

styrofoam, 2¼" thick. For the cab, cut to 3" x 3", cut two for trailer 2½" x 4". Ice with royal icing.

3. Bake a Loaf cake for cab and one in the Long loaf pan for trailer. Carve loaf cake as diagram shows. Set cab and trailer on wax paper, close together. Trace around truck to make pattern for cardboard base. Cut out base and reassemble truck on it. Ice supports to foil-covered board and attach truck to supports with icing.

4. Pipe grille with tube 2B. Attach windows with icing and outline doors with tube 2. Pipe stripes with tube 1D, grooving for doors. Pipe, and over-pipe twice, curves for fenders with tube 6. Now cover truck with tube 14 stars. Attach bumpers and headlights with icing. Secure wheels and hubcaps to side of cab, and to supports under trailer. Add a tube 2 message. We figure piped the horns and exhaust pipes in royal icing on wax paper. Antenna is an iced toothpick.

Serve his 18-wheeler to 24, cutting trailer into 16 pieces, cab into eight.

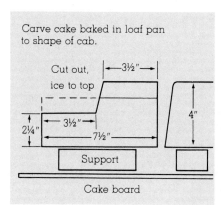

Carve cake baked in loaf pan to shape of cab.

His **O**ccupation: master of an 18-wheeler

P is for that universal celebration, St. Patrick's day! _Practical_ readers share _Profit-making_ tips

Call up the neighbors, put on the green and wear your dancing shoes!

The cheeriest couple that ever danced a jig!

Put their picture on a cake top, filled in with tinted poured fondant.

1. Pipe royal icing shamrocks with tubes 101 and 104 and set aside to dry. Bake, fill and ice a two-layer 11" x 15" sheet cake. Divide long sides of cake into sevenths, short sides into fifths and mark 1" up from base.

2. Transfer _Celebrate!_ pattern to cake top. Outline with tube 2 and royal icing. Make a recipe of Quick poured fondant, tint small amounts flesh color, brown and gold. Tint half the remainder pale green, half deeper green. Keep fondant covered and over hot water as you work. Fill in areas with tube 2. Let fondant crust, then mix food color with one or two teaspoons of any white liqueur and paint cheeks. Pipe eyes, mouths and stripes on socks with tube 1, noses with tube 4, buttons with tubes 5 and 2. Do shamrock print on skirt and kerchief with tube 3, white ruffle with tube 101.

3. Pipe tube 16 shell borders at bottom and top of cake. Do tube 104 ruffles from mark to mark and top with swags piped with same tube. Attach larger shamrocks to points. Print a tube 2 message on cake top, add small shamrocks. Serve to 35 merry-makers.

Happy St. Pat's

A _Quick & Pretty_ cake, trimmed and tinted for the occasion.

1. Mold small and tiny green hearts in Candy Melts™ confectionery coating. Bake, fill and ice a two-layer 12" petal cake and a single-layer 6" petal tier.

2. On 12" cake, pipe a tube 16 bottom shell border. Add elongated tube 19 curved shells on each curve, then a fleur-de-lis.

With same tube, pipe curved shells at edge of cake top and finish with upright shells and a star.

3. Pipe tube 1 message on top tier. Decorate in similar fashion to lower tier. Pipe bottom shell border with tube 14, curved shells with tube 17. Arrange trios of hearts on lower tier top to form shamrocks. Attach tiny hearts to side of tier. Serve to 29 guests.

Readers tell how to make Profits on cake decorating

Many thanks to all of you who generously shared your experiences. To sum up all of your advice—"please your customer and the profits will come". To each of you whose suggestion is printed here we are sending a $25.00 check and our congratulations.

I total my cost for all ingredients and everything needed for baking and decorating a cake. Then I double it. This is my profit, plus the experience and decorating fun. *Diane Thibodeaux*, Louisiana.

I clip out the engagement announcements that are in my local paper. Then I send the bride-to-be a business card and letter telling about my wedding cake business. I have had great response. *Vicki Hall*, California.

Most people are scared to touch wedding cakes, let alone move or cut them—so my price *includes* moving, assembly, cutting, serving, clean up and removing. *Mrs. Lee O. Connor*, N. Carolina.

Hold an open house: choose a date close to a major holiday. Invite friends, neighbors, (tell them to bring a friend). Serve samples of your cakes. Have a display of seasonal cakes which may be purchased. You'll sell everything and get plenty of orders. *Linda Thomson*, Massachusetts.

In order to take more orders on a given day, make your frosting, flowers, and grease your pans ahead of time. Pack the fountain and all that goes with large cakes several days before delivery. *Audrey Reed*, Illinois

Make a "care box" to take with you for delivery. Permanent items may include ribbon, wires, scissors, disposable bags, spatula, a few basic tubes, straight pins, tape. Add icing at the last minute. This can get you through many tight spots. *Y. Blush*, Colorado.

Have customers pick up all-occasion cakes and deliver only large tiered cakes. Charge an additional fee for far distances. *Mrs. Bob E. Larance*, Texas.

Sell related services—customers ordering cakes are usually interested in buying mints or candies to go with their order. *Mari Herzog*, Michigan.

Do all your baking at one time. Schedule your baking for the week on one day. Heating the oven every day will give your profits to the utility company. Two ovens are a time saver. *Becky Boyde*, Pennsylvania.

Use a friend as a back-up. She will do the same for you. You won't lose business this way, you'll keep it, because you won't have to disappoint a customer. *Meg Meehan*, New York.

I have a cake expense sheet I fill out to help me keep track of my expenses. Being aware of all incurred expenses is an extremely important part of making a profit. Be sure to record your time. *Jo Beth Harry*, Oregon.

I take the orders ahead of time, make the cakes and freeze them. Then, I start an assembly line for decorating. Much easier than doing them one at a time! *Carolyn A. Ellis*, Texas.

I look though my *Celebrate!* books for outstanding ideas for color flow and gum paste cake toppers. People really like them. *Elizabeth Eaton*, Idaho.

For customers who don't know what theme they want on a cake, I suggest a cake that looks like a wrapped present, complete with a large bow. It's both dessert and gift! *Sauly Anderson*, California.

Be creative! be professional! People come to me to get a cake they can't buy from a bakery. Be original. Bake with quality ingredients. Use a foil-covered cake board, tuk-n-ruffle, white boxes. *Connie Kruelle*, Maryland.

Use cookies, candies, sugar molds to decorate your cakes. They are inexpensive and a big help. *Cil Fortman*, New York.

I always call my customers a day or two after delivery to be sure they're satisfied. A satisfied customer is a repeat customer. *Yvonne Grandel*, San Francisco.

My son's second grade teacher asked parents to demonstrate their jobs to the class. I baked and partially iced a Cookie Monster cake. I let each student help put the "fur" on Cookie Monster. The students really enjoyed it! Since then, I have been asked to decorate cakes for the school personnel's birthdays. *Mrs. Pat Shear*, Wisconsin.

For 95% response to my candy making demonstrations, I use this method. I run a newspaper ad requesting readers to call. I explain to them that they must come to my shop in advance and pay a $5.00 fee. I then give them a $3.00 coupon for free merchandise, to be selected on the day of the class. I make enough to pay for the ad. *Dolores McCann*, Ohio.

I present tiny pastel sugar bells to brides for coffee. A solid sugar bell is the equivalent of two teaspoons of sugar; a hollowed sugar bell is one. It's amazing how the guests enjoy that special, elegant touch. For wedding showers I make umbrellas, for baby showers, booties. *Iris O. Barno*, Texas.

The biggest reason I sell a lot of candy and cakes is samples. Last Valentine's day a one pound sample box gave me 75 orders! *Susan J. Spohr*, California.

I send a small cake serving chart with my sheet and wedding cakes. *Elizabeth Tabaka*, Ohio.

Customers appreciate the caution I put on cake boxes. "Break box down and *slide* cake out. Do not lift out or frosting may crease." *Nancy Joy*, New Hampshire.

I give free demonstrations for clubs and youth groups. I take along disposable bags, icing and tubes. They all try their hand at decorating. I always see some of them in my shop after that, wanting to do cakes of their own. *Betty Rathbun*, Michigan.

I typed out a flyer about my business, with a dollar-off coupon. We distributed several hundred copies to neighbors and apartment complexes. Orders started coming in that very day! *Janet Goldenbogen*, New York.

If you decorate wedding cakes, do not meet directly with the bride. Line up one or more caterers to work with. Prepare a complete list of sizes, prices, basic styles and choices of ornaments. Give this information and pictures to the caterer. He will be meeting with the bride anyhow, and can get all the information for the cake order. This saves the bride and you valuable time. *Jean Adams*, Indiana.

I only order pans and special tubes when I have a cake order that calls for their use, so I never waste money on unneeded equipment. I do keep a few wedding ornaments for last minute orders. *Annette Holden*, Kentucky.

When I deliver a cake I bring a bag of royal icing flowers with it, then suggest to the customer that she place a flower on each piece she serves. This helps promote my sales. *Lucille Kollarits*, Illinois.

In addition to bridal shops, florist, jewelry and formal wear stores all will help promote wedding cake sales. Make an attractive dummy cake for display. It will draw in customers and the store will be happy to recommend you. *Donna L. Taylor*, Illinois.

Charge a set amount for each serving. It will help to simplify your figuring. *Caroline Goodbaudy*, California.

Personalize each cake. Check age, hobbies, favorite color, occupation and give a wide choice of flavors. This gets repeat orders. *Bettye Chumney*, Tennessee.

The first year I was into cake decorating (just before Easter), I gave a decorated egg minicake to each child in our neighborhood. I made the children very happy and received many cake orders. *Shirley G. Baine*, Georgia.

When I started decorating, I visited offices where my relatives worked. Now five of these offices keep me busy doing cakes. I also do shower cakes for a local caterer. *Cindy Goolsby*, Texas.

Check out Health Department regulations before working with any food product and selling it from your home. Regulations vary in every area—and by checking them first you may very well avoid a large fine for not complying. *Gail Wiedenbeck*, Wisconsin.

Check with the florist who is arranging the wedding flowers, so the flowers on the cake can carry out the color scheme. Add the same flowers to the cutting knife and toasting glasses. *Terri Reese*, California.

For delivering cakes locally I never charge a fee, but I do give the bride a self-addressed, stamped envelope and request that she mail me a photographer's picture of the cake. *Louise Sharp*, Washington.

A gum paste plaque for an Eagle Scout or a baby carriage of gum paste for a new mother are touches that add a third dimension to the cake—and to profits. *Esther G. Lyon*, Connecticut.

When a bride requests a very large cake for only 100 to 150 guests, use cake dummies as the base tiers. These give the effect of a large cake and the cost of ingredients is kept at a minimum for a better profit. *Irene Pagano*, New Jersey.

I make it easy for out-of-town parents to provide birthday cakes for their children attending our local college. In late summer, the college sends a form to the parents stating that a 9" x 13" cake can be ordered for delivery on the student's birthday. There's a choice of flavors and three types of decoration plus greeting. A secretary picks up the cakes at my home and I am mailed a check each month. *Virginia McMacken*, Michigan.

Spend a few cents, gain new customers—thus more profit! Use colored foil to cover cake boards, bags for lollipops, candy boxes and cups for candy, white boxes for cakes. People will tell others, "her work looks so professional!" *Bonnie Kovatch*, Colorado.

Never over decorate, keep it simple. Make it neat. The flavor and moistness of a cake is very important. A nice smile helps when the customer picks up the cake. *Josephine Mosbrucker*, North Dakota.

Here's a tip for a good picture: take the cake outdoors, out of direct sunlight. *Miracle Moore*, Arizona.

is for Quick & Pretty cakes . . .
flowery, fast, lovely enough
for your nicest party

Spring tulips

Pipe them right on a graceful oval cake. Use buttercream to ice the cake and for all trim.

1. Bake, fill and ice a two-layer 9″ oval cake. Place on serving tray and edge base with rosettes piped with tube 18.

2. Pipe tube 13 stems on cake top. The flowers are just three shells piped with tube 199. First pipe a center shell at end of stem, drawing out to a point. Now pipe a shell on either side, points curving sharply outward. Pipe center leaf first. Outline a long pointed oval with tube 13, then fill in with more lines. Do two side leaves, extending them right over the curved edge of the cake. Complete border with tube 362 shells. Serve with pride to twelve.

Quick & Pretty
Summer sunflowers

1. Ice a single-layer 12″ petal cake with Chocolate buttercream. Pipe a tube 68 shell motion base border. Edge top with tube 16 shells. Use a 2⅜″ round cookie cutter to pattern the flowers. Lightly press a circle within one curve of the cake top, about 1″ in from the edge. Skip a curve, then mark another circle. Repeat on other side of cake.

2. Pipe tube 14 stems from circles, extending down sides of cake. Pipe a ring around each circle with tube 12, then fill in with a spiral piped with same tube.

Surround with leafy petals piped with tube 70. Fill in centers with tube 14 stars, then pipe a circle of tube 2 yellow dots. Finish your show-off cake with tube 112 leaves. Serve to twelve.

Quick & Pretty
A big ruffled flower

1. Bake, fill and ice a two-layer 9″ petal cake. Pipe shell borders at bottom and top with tube 16. Drop string guidelines for ruffles on side, starting about 1½″ up at each indentation.

2. Following guidelines, pipe tube 124 ruffles on cake side. Pipe outer ruffles, then inner ruffles on cake

top, following curves of cake. Finish with tube 101 bows. This flowery little cake serves eight.

Quick & Pretty
A spray of daisies

1. Bake, fill and ice a two-layer 7″ x 11″ sheet cake. Pipe stems on cake top with tube 13. Tube 15 does all the rest of the decorating.

2. On each corner at base of cake, pipe radiating shell petals. Center with a rosette. Complete border with shells. Edge top of cake with a shell border. Now pipe daisies on cake top with shell petals centered by rosettes. Add a few green leaves. Serve to 18.

A Quick & Pretty cake in a Quilt design

The glorious rolling star is reproduced on a striking cake that's remarkably quick and easy to decorate.

1. Bake and fill a two-layer 12" square cake. Using *Celebrate!* pattern, trim off corners to octagon shape. Ice with Snow-white buttercream. Transfer star pattern to cake top. Divide each side of cake in half and mark at base. Connect marks with corners to form triangles.

2. Outline rolling star pattern with tube 3. Remember to pipe lines around outside of pattern as well as interior lines. Now make a recipe of Quick poured fondant. Heat it to about 105°F, so it is of a thin consistency. Tint yellow. Fill in outer areas with tube 5 and a quick back-and-forth movement so fondant fills evenly. To remaining fondant, add orange liquid color to achieve a light orange. Add drops of hot water, if necessary, for a pourable consistency. Fill in four diamond shapes with tube 5 and a back-and-forth movement.

Finally, add a little red liquid color to remaining fondant for a red-orange color. Thin with drops of hot water as needed. Fill in remaining diamonds.

3. Let fondant stiffen to piping consistency, and pipe tube 3 dots within all triangles. Complete the trim by piping tube 13 shell borders. Serve your glorious rolling star to 32.

Pretty sheet cakes done a Quick new way

Start with an easy-to-serve sheet cake. Cover it quickly with buttercream, using giant tube 789. Add fast, interesting borders—garnish with flowers from your made-ahead supply. You've created a pretty cake, decorated in just minutes!

The yellow cake is a single-layer 9" x 13" sheet. Cover long sides first with tube 789, curving slightly around corners. Mark center of cake at top edges of short sides. Now cover cake, doing side edges first, then two center strips. Start at base of one short side, move across top and end at base of opposite side. Fill spaces between strips with tube 125

"pleating", using a shell motion. Run a tube 7 line around base of cake and cover with matching pleating. Arrange flowers in a curve on mounds of icing. Trim with tube 66 leaves and serve to twelve guests.

The pink cake is a petite 7" x 11", one layer. First cover long sides with tube 789, curving slightly around corners. Now cover short sides and top, starting with one edge of cake, then doing opposite edge. Finally pipe an icing strip down center of cake. Fill in between strips with tube 1D. Attach neat rows of drop flowers and tube 66 leaves. Complete with a tube 16 base shell border.

Serves nine guests.

The big two-color cake, a single-layer 12" x 18", gives guests a choice! Divide cake in halves on all four sides and connect marks to divide in fourths. Do chocolate areas first, starting at center marks and piping three evenly-spaced tube 789 strips across top. Fill in spaces with tube 47. Complete pink areas the same way. Now add the ruffly tube 125 borders. Hold narrow end of tube straight up, and move from base of sides to top center. Do bottom border the same way. Attach sprays of drop flowers and add tube 66 leaves. Serve to 26.

121

 is for <u>Retirement</u>. Celebrate this happy occasion with a splendid cake!

Free at last! The years of day-by-day work are over. Now the retiree is free to pursue the interests dearest to her heart. Have a party! Center the table with a cake as happy as the occasion.

Rainbow

A brilliant arch curves over an easy-to-serve square cake.

1. Bake the rainbow with a firm pound cake recipe in the Horseshoe pan. (This will take five cups of batter. Average mix yields 3½ cups.) Chill the cake, then measure 6″ up from each outer end of horseshoe. Trim off to make an arch. Attach cake boards, cut same size and shape, to ends of arch.

2. Carve two pine trees from cut-off ends of horseshoe. Cut in triangles about 4½″ high, 3″ wide at base. Round off to tree shapes. Attach each to a tiny cake board cut the same size and shape as base. Pipe spaced tube 75 shells on trees for branches. Starting at bottom, pull out tube 75 "needles".

Pipe drop flowers in royal icing with tubes 35 and 27. Add tube 2 centers and dry.

3. Bake and fill a two-layer 10″ square cake. Ice top with green buttercream and rough up with a spatula. Ice sides smoothly in white. Write message on sides of cake with tube 2. Pipe a tube 18 rosette bottom border, a tube 16 top shell border.

4. Tint buttercream for rainbow. We chose violet, blue, green, yellow and red as a facsimile of the real rainbow. Lay arch on its side and fill in inner curve with tube 16 violet stars. Set arch upright and center on cake top diagonally. Starting at base of inner curve, pipe a row of tube 16 violet stars. Repeat twice more for three parallel rows. Do other colors the same, always piping three parallel rows for an even effect. Continue until entire rainbow is covered with stars.

5. Set trees in position, one on either side of rainbow. Attach drop flowers in clusters and trim with tube 65 leaves. Pipe patches of grass with tube 2. Your rainbow cake is beautiful from every angle. Serve square cake to 20 guests. Lay rainbow on its side and cut into eight pieces. Want a larger cake to serve a crowd? Set rainbow on a big sheet cake. It will look just as showy.

124

Retirement cakes show happy times ahead

For the passionate gardener

Now she'll have time to grow prize-winning flowers! Mold her replica in gum paste even weeks ahead—then just before the party, decorate the cake. All patterns needed are in *Celebrate!* patterns or the People Mold booklet.

1. Make flower basket and trowel, using the recipe on page 36. For basket, roll out gum paste about 1/16" thick. Cut with pattern and dry within smallest curved former. Roll a little rope of gum paste about 2½" long for handle, attach with egg white to basket and prop with cotton balls to dry. Fill with drop flowers, secured with royal icing. For trowel, model a little ¾" cylinder for handle, cut blade from thinly rolled gum paste and attach with egg white. Prop with cotton balls to dry.

2. For the figure, use the woman mold from the People mold set. Refer to page 110 and the booklet that comes with the molds for directions. Make up the face, then attach upper body to lower body. Allow to dry, dress figure in thinly rolled gum paste. First pants, then bodice, using patterns. Mold arms, then hold to body to bend to position. Prop to dry. Attach sleeves, then secure trowel in hand, basket on arm with tiny pieces of gum paste dipped in egg white. Attach arms to body the same way. Prop completed figure to dry. Paint stripes on shirt with food color and pipe royal icing hair with tube 13.

3. Cut oval plaque from gum paste rolled ⅛" thick. Hold figure above it to determine position of holes for wires on feet. Make holes with a pointed stick and dry flat.

4. Pipe royal icing drop flowers with tubes 129 and 225. Dry. Bake, fill and ice a two-layer 9" x 13" cake. Write message on cake

top with tube 1. Divide long sides of cake into fifths, short sides into fourths and mark at base. Pipe clusters of stems with tube 1, attach flowers and add tube 65 leaves. Pipe tube 16 shell border at base and top of cake. Cut an oval of plastic wrap, using plaque pattern, lay on cake top, then put gum paste plaque on top. Secure figure to plaque with tiny pieces of gum paste dipped in egg white and pushing wires on feet through holes. Trim with a curve of flowers. Cake serves 24. Lift off figure to present to the retiree.

Quick & Pretty
Sunshine coming!

Serve this cheery cake at the retirement party to reflect the joy of the occasion.

1. Pipe royal icing drop flowers with tubes 2F, and 193. Pipe tube 2 centers and dry.

2. Bake, fill and ice a two-layer 12" petal cake. Transfer pattern for sun. Outline pattern with tube 3 and a mixture of half royal icing, half piping gel. Write message with tube 1 and the same mixture.

3. Fill in sun design with piping gel and tube 3 dots. Pipe tube 3 stems, attach flowers and add tube 65 leaves. Pipe tube 15 shell borders at base and top. Pipe curved scrolls at base of cake with tube 20. Serve to 26 guests.

cakes graced with birds and blossoms
and with flowery <u>Shower</u> cakes

A scarlet cardinal perches on a pussy willow

What could say "Spring" more sweetly! The beautiful Color Flow plaque is lifted off before serving to present to the guest of honor.

1. Make the plaque. Tape *Celebrate!* pattern smoothly to glass or plexiglass (never use cardboard—it will draw moisture from the icing and warp). Tape wax paper smoothly over the pattern. Outline the double circles with tube 6, stopping after each quarter curve to assure a perfect complete circle. Thin the icing by stirring in drops of water. When a spoonful of icing dropped in the batch disappears at a count of twelve, the consistency is correct. Fill in the areas with tube 4, leaving a little space next to outlines so icing will flow in perfectly flat. Pipe divisions on circles with tube 6. Dry thoroughly. Transfer pussy willow pattern to plaque. Pipe design with royal icing. Do branches with oval tube 55, holding long side of opening against surface, pussy willows with tube 3, brown pods with tube 3. When icing sets up, cover pussy willows with tube OL dots.

2. Do bird separately. Tape pattern to glass or plexiglass, tape wax paper over it and outline all areas with tube 2. Thin the icing, using a count of 15 for consistency test, and flow in the areas, using tube 3 for larger spaces, tube 1 for small spaces. Let icing build up for rounded effect. When thoroughly dry, pipe wing, tail feathers and crest with tube 101s. Pipe support lines for bird on plaque with tube 4. Over-pipe twice with same tube, dry, then pipe a dot of icing on each support and set bird in position. Pipe claws with tube 3 and smooth onto legs with a damp brush.

3. Prepare cake. Bake a 14" base bevel, a 10" round layer and a 10" top bevel, using a firm pound cake recipe. Fill, ice with buttercream, then cover with rolled fondant. You will need two recipes. Divide cake into sixths and mark at base of 10" layer. Transfer pussy willow pattern at marks and pipe the same as on plaque. Add a tube 3 bulb border, then a tube 102 shell motion "pleated" border at edge.

4. Mark a 7" circle on cake top and pipe a tube 5 royal icing ring. Let dry, then top with spaced icing dots and set plaque in position. Serve to 24.

Spring's tulips, in candy!

1. Make tulips and leaves as shown on page 68. You will need a dozen tulips. Paint a plastic bowl with thinned royal icing to match cake. Fill with a half-ball of styrofoam, cover ball with icing, then arrange leaves and flowers.

2. Bake, fill and ice a two-layer 10" square cake and a single-layer 6" round. Assemble on cake board. Divide top edges of square tier into fifths. Starting 1" in from each corner, divide base of cake into fourths.

3. Pipe tube 16 shell borders at base of square tier and at base and top of round tier. Pipe tube 17 zigzag garlands from mark to mark at bottom, then add tube 16 rosettes. Drop tube 13 double strings from mark to mark at top of tier, then pipe tube 14 shells and stars. Finish with a tube 16 top shell border. Arrange candy stems, leaves and tulips on top of tier, then set bowl in position. Serve to 23.

Glorify a sheet cake for a Shower

Goldfinch in a flowery nest

1. Use Figure piping icing for nest and birds. For nest, cut a 3½" circle from 1" thick styrofoam. Ice, then circle edge with two tube 12 lines. Top with a tube 8 line, then cover with tube 3 "straw". Scatter with tube 13 drop flowers. Do birds on wax paper. Pipe body as a tube 2A shell. Insert tube 5 into small end of shell and pipe a ball-shaped head. Let set up, then add tube 101s wings and tail, tube 2 eyes and tube 3 beak. Trim fronts of wings with tube 1s "V"s. Brush brown icing on head.

2. Pipe tube 224 drop flowers and dry. Bake, fill and ice a two-layer 9" x 13" cake. Measuring 4" in from each corner, mark triangles on top and sides. Mark circles in centers of long sides with a 2½" cutter. Mark hearts on corners with a 2⅛" cutter. Pipe message with tube 1.

3. Pipe a tube 16 bottom shell border. Do all other decorating with tube 14. Attach flower clusters in hearts and circles, then pipe tube 65 leaves. Set the little nest on cake top and add the birds on mounds of icing. Present it to the bride-to-be before serving to 24.

Quick & Pretty

Parasols for a shower party

1. Pipe many tubes 107 and 224 drop flowers in royal icing and dry. Mount some on toothpick stems. Paint plastic parasols with thinned royal icing, trim with ribbon bows and flowers.

2. Bake, fill and ice a two-layer 9" x 13" cake. Mark top by pressing with an oval pan. Fill in with green icing and rough with a spatula. Write message on side with tube 1. Pipe a tube 68 shell-motion border at base, a tube 16 shell border at top. Edge oval with tube 14 shells. Mound icing at corners and press in flowers in cascades. Plant flowers in oval and push in parasols. Serve to 24.

Bells ring out the news

A big cake for a large party, but very dainty and fresh with its spring flowers and quick lacy trims.

1. Pipe royal icing flowers in advance. Do daffodils with tube 124 petals, pinched to a point, tube 4 spiral cups and tube 1 ruffly edges. Pipe violets with tube 102 and add tube 1 centers. Wire satin bows to toothpicks.

2. Bake, fill and ice a two-layer 12" x 18" cake. Divide long sides into sixths, short sides into fourths and mark at top edge. Drop string guidelines for garlands. Bake two single-layer bell cakes, ice with buttercream and cover with poured fondant. Lightly mark position of bell cakes on sheet cake top with a bell pan. Write names with tube 1.

3. Pipe tube 4 bulb borders on bell cakes. Pipe quick triple scallops with tube 89. Set on sheet cake top. On sheet cake, pipe a tube 172 shell border and trim with tube 18 stars. Fill in area from string guidelines to bell cakes with tube 1 sotas (see page 98). Pipe ruffled zigzag garlands with tube 98. Now pose the flowers on mounds of icing and add the satin bows. Serve to 66 guests.

 is for <u>Thanksgiving.</u> Create a "hand-embroidered" cake to celebrate! Decorate a <u>Teacher's</u> cake, a pretty <u>Telephone</u> cake, or a quick <u>Thank you</u> cake.

Give thanks

Warm autumn colors and decorating techniques that recall an old-fashioned sampler create a cake very much in the spirit of the holiday.

1. Bake and fill a two-layer 9" x 13" sheet cake. Ice smoothly in buttercream. Transfer *Celebrate!* patterns to top and sides. Set on serving tray.

2. Start by doing "satin-stitch" pattern for leaves on one side of cake. Use royal icing for all "embroidery". Do light green half of leaf by laying down parallel, touching strokes of tube 1 icing from edge to center. Repeat, using deeper green icing for other half of leaf. Pipe tiny bulbs for center vein.

3. For flower, pipe slender tube 1 loops extending from edge of smallest circle to outer edge of largest circle on pattern. Change to a lighter colored icing and pipe a second series of loops from center point of pattern to edge of second circle. Fill in smallest circle with tube 1s dots, like French knots. Complete designs on all four sides of cake.

4. On top of cake, do lettering first with tube 1s. Be precise in starting and stopping the diagonal strokes for a neat effect. Do leaves and flowers with tube 1, using same method as you used on side designs. To make the work go quickly, do inner light green areas of all leaves first, then go back and do outer areas of all leaves in deeper green. Pipe flowers just as you did those in side designs, doing all piping of one color at a time.

5. Pipe a tailored tube 2B border at base of cake. On upper edge, pipe a line of tube 1s "cross stitching". Pipe a tiny "V", then pipe an inverted "V" on top of it. Use ridges in the tube 2B border to guide the size of the cross stitch. Continue around cake.

6. On top of cake, pipe a tube 2B border at edge. At corners, cut off the icing strips with a knife for a mitred effect. Trim inner edge of border with tube 1s cross stitching, just as you did for bottom border. Serve this skillful masterpiece to 24 guests.

A big red apple . . .

is a perfect way to tell a teacher how much you appreciate her efforts. It's even more delicious than the real thing!

1. Bake a firm pound cake in the 6" ball pan and fill the two halves with buttercream. Flatten the base so it stands upright and carve out an indentation for stem. Ice with buttercream.

2. Make half the Candy for Flowers recipe on page 98 for covering the cake. Take out a tiny amount and tint green for leaves. Take a second tiny portion and tint brown for stem. Tint remainder red. Follow the directions on page 98 to cover the cake. This is the perfect way to cover a ball. The mixture is so pliable it's easy to smooth over the curves. Cut the leaves with the small violet cutter from the Flower garden cutter set and harden overnight in curved form. Roll a little rope with your hands for stem. Attach to apple and present to teacher. Cake serves twelve.

A pretty pink telephone

Here's a cake for the friend who calls so often or for a talkative teenager. The telephone is easily carved from an oval cake.

1. Make a half-recipe of marzipan for touch-tone panel and flowers. Tint half pink, half yellow. Roll out pink marzipan to ¼" thickness and cut a rectangle, 2½" x 3¾", for panel. Roll out yellow marzipan to ¼" thickness and cut twelve ½" squares for buttons. Attach buttons to panel. From remaining marzipan cut flowers with the Flower garden violet cutter and attach centers cut with tube 9. Let harden, then glaze.

2. Bake, fill and ice a two-layer 10" round cake. Bake a single-layer 9" oval pound cake for the telephone.

to say "Thanks"

Chill, then carve as diagram shows. Slant the base from 2" high at back to 1½" high at front. Cover top of base with tube 14 stars, then center touch-tone panel. Cover inner side of receiver with stars, then place on base. Set telephone on 10" cake, then complete covering with stars.

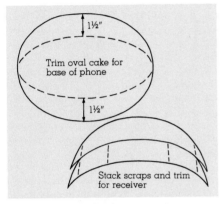

3. Pipe a tube 4B shell border at base of cake and add tube 13 scallops. Do top shell border with tube 504. Pipe greeting and loops for cord with tube 14. Trim cake with flowers. Serve cake to 14, telephone to four .

Quick & Pretty
Say "Thank you" sweetly

1. Pipe many royal icing drop flowers with tube 107, add tube 2 centers and dry.

2. Bake, fill and ice a two-layer 8" square cake. Cover with poured fondant. Lightly mark a circle on cake top with a 6" pan. Mark curves on each side with a 10" round pan.

3. Write message with tube 2. Pipe four tube 102 bows on marked circle, then attach flowers to complete circle. Outline curves on sides with flowers, then fill in area to base with flowers. Pipe bows at corners. Trim curves with tube 65 leaves. Serve this pretty thank you note to ten.

is for <u>Unicorn.</u> Decorate an <u>Unusual</u> showpiece cake that features this fanciful creature

The unicorn is the most fascinating of the fabled beasts of folklore. For many centuries everyone believed that it *did* exist. People reported they had seen unicorns in India, Persia, Albyssinia, Scandinavia, Tibet and Poland—and in Maine, Florida and Canada! Artists of many nationalities have depicted the unicorn in paintings, woodcuts, enamels and tapestries.

In literature, drinking from a unicorn's horn was said to make a person immune to illness or even poison. The Chinese believed the unicorn would bring good fortune and long life. In the Old Testament, its pedigree went back to Adam and Eve! In Christian symbolism, the unicorn makes poisoned water pure by dipping his horn into it. He is a symbol of purity and strength, right and might.

Add to the legends of the unicorn by decorating this showpiece cake. Here he gambols playfully in a flowery field.

The showpiece cake

1. Do the unicorn in Color Flow. Because this is a large piece, the work is done directly on a gum paste plaque. Roll out the blue gum paste (recipe, page 36) to about ⅛" thickness, using *Celebrate!* pattern. Roll out the green gum paste thin as possible for the hill, and attach, while wet, to the blue plaque with egg white. Dry thoroughly, then transfer the unicorn pattern to the plaque.

2. Outline with tube 2 and Color Flow icing straight from the batch. Let outlines set up, then fill in with thinned icing a little thicker than usual for a rounded, dimensional effect. Drop a small spoonful into the icing. When it disappears at the count of 15 it is at about the correct consistency. Dry thoroughly.

3. Pipe many tiny drop flowers with tube 13, center with tube 1s and dry. Pipe the unicorn's flowing mane and tail with tube 1s. Add his blue teardrop eye with tube 3. Almost cover the wreath around his neck with flowers, attaching with dots of icing. Add tiny tube 65s leaves. Cover the green hill with flowers and leaves the same way. Edge the plaque with tube 3 beading, then go back and pipe a

projecting bead between every fourth and fifth bead already piped. Dry.

4. Bake and fill a two-layer 10" x 4" square cake. Chill, then trim top to level. Ice in ivory buttercream. (Use butter instead of shortening to achieve the creamy color.) Mark pattern for curves on cake sides.

5. Outline the marked curves in green icing and tube 5. Now fill in entire area between curves and base of cake with tube 2B and green icing. Smooth with a small spatula. Fill in area from curves to base with the tiny drop flowers.

6. Pipe an upright shell column with tube 22 at each corner, up to marked curve. Following marks, pipe tube 124 swags. Top with tube 5 fleurs-de-lis. Pipe a tube 6 bulb border around top edge of cake. Pipe two curved shells at each corner, meeting at column. Add a star where they join. Pipe tube 65s leaves among the flowers.

7. Pipe mounds of icing and let set up to support the plaque in position. Serve your beautiful unicorn showpiece to 20 guests. The plaque is beautiful enough to be framed.

 is for <u>Valentine's</u> day... a time to show your love in very special ways

It's easy for a decorator to display her affection! One of the nicest ways is to give a sensational love party for the children. Serve their favorite foods, then dress them up to suit the Valentine theme.

Pizza is always a winner! Use your favorite recipe for the dough. Roll out, then mark with the largest cookie cutter from the Heart set. Cut out the shapes with a sharp knife, pile on the toppings and bake. (You can do this with a purchased frozen pizza, too.)

Valentine salads are molded from red fruit-flavored gelatin in the heart cupcake pan. Garnish with a piped mayonnaise heart.

Mark each place with a 3-D candy heart for a take-home treasure. Mold from Candy Melts™ confectionery coating, using the color contrast method, page 34, for the dainty trim. Pipe their names with royal icing thinned with piping gel and add red bows.

Dessert is really special! Mold strawberry ice cream in the Heart cupcake pan, pipe a big whipped cream heart with tube 172, then crown with molded candy hearts.

The glorious Valentine cake is the centerpiece. Turn the page for decorating directions.

Hearts and flowers, ribbons and roses, all come together on this Valentine centerpiece. The frilly cake is quickly decorated, the red hearts are made of gum paste, and the dainty fabric flowers are pretty time-savers.

1. Make trims ahead. Tint gum paste, page 36, and cut the hearts with Miniature and Truffle cutters. Dry, then attach florists' wire stems to backs of hearts with royal icing for bouquets. Edge hearts for lower tier sides with tube 1 beading and royal icing. Fill a Heart bowl with a styrofoam ball, ice to secure and arrange flowers and hearts for large bouquet.

Make eight clusters of tiny stemmed hearts and flowers by twisting stems together.

2. Bake, fill and ice the petal-shaped tiers—a two-layer 12″ and a single-layer 6″. Assemble on serving tray.

3. On base tier, pipe a tube 16 bottom shell border. Pipe a tube 22 upright shell and a tube 16 star at each indentation. Drop string guidelines, then pipe tube 126 ruffles. Top with tube 18 zigzag garlands and curved shells. On top of tier, pipe facing tube 22 curved shells.

On top tier, pipe a tube 16 bottom

shell border, then tube 104 ruffles and tube 14 rosettes. On top edge, pipe tube 16 curved shells centered with upright shells. Add tube 14 stars.

4. Now add the hearts and flowers. Insert a Flower spike in the center of each curve of the base tier. Fill with heart-and-flower clusters. Attach beaded hearts to tier sides. Set bouquet on cake top and garnish with a pink satin bow. Serve this impressive Valentine to 29 party guests. The flower arrangements are take-home favors.

The glorious Valentine cake
shown on page 136

It's the sweetest, cutest, happiest cake you could make for a party!

1. Prepare ornament. Use Roll-out cookie dough to cut a boy and a girl with cutters from the Christmas set. Also cut a tiny 1″ heart. Lay popsicle sticks on a cookie sheet, lay cookies on them, ends of sticks extending, and bake. (Cut remaining dough into heart shapes for Valentine treats.) Use the Color Flow technique to trim the cookies. Outline areas with tube 1, then fill in with thinned icing. Add features and details with tube 2. For an all-around view, turn over and outline and fill in again.

2. The Color Flow technique does the lettering, too. Tape *Celebrate!*

patterns to a 12″ curved form and tape wax paper over them. Outline with tube 1, then fill in letters and hearts with thinned icing.

3. Bake, fill and ice a two-layer 12″ round tier and a single-layer 6″ heart tier. Assemble on serving tray and pipe the ruffly sweet pea borders. Use tube 125. On base of lower tier, pipe a petal against tier side, then an upright petal, and last, a petal on tray. Continue around cake. Do top border and base border on upper tier the same way. Change to tube 124 to do top border on top tier. Push sticks on ornament into top tier. Center the cake on the party table and wait for applause! Cut bottom tier into 22 pieces, top tier into 3.

Quick & Pretty
**Chocolate-dipped
strawberries**

Out of this world! For real luxury,
dip the berries in tempered milk
chocolate (page 143). For an even
quicker treat, dip in chocolate-
flavored confectionery coating.
Make this delicate treat the
day you plan to serve it.

Choose perfect, unblemished
berries. Carefully wash and dry
them. Holding by the stem, dip the
berries into tempered chocolate or
melted coating, leaving top of
berry uncovered. Place on wax
paper-covered cookie sheet. Slide
cookie sheet into refrigerator for
five minutes only, then complete
hardening at room temperature.
One pound of chocolate or coating
will cover about 40 berries. Store
a few hours at room temperature.

The ultimate love cake

1. Make the candy wild roses and
leaves ahead of time (page 69).

2. Bake and fill a two-layer 9″
heart cake and a single-layer 6″
heart. Ice with buttercream. Cover
small heart with pink-tinted
poured fondant, large heart with
chocolate poured fondant.
Assemble on serving tray.

3. Write "Love" on cake top with
tube 1. Borders are made of the
same Candy for Flowers formula
as the flowers. Form a rough
cylinder of the mixture and roll
into a long rope. Start by rolling
on surface with your two hands in
center of cylinder. As it thins,
move your hands outward until
you have a long rope about ¼″ in
diameter. Wrap the rope around
the top tier, clip off and press ends
together smoothly. For border on
lower tier, "braid" two ropes.
Attach flowers and leaves with
dots of royal icing. Serve to 15.

Nothing's too good for your Valentine!

A beautiful...and delicious... alentine gift box

Would you like to give a special valentine a very special gift? Mold this candy box in Candy Melts™ confectionery coating, trim it with candy roses, then fill it with brandied cherries!

1. Make roses and leaves from confectionery coating. Page 69 shows just how to model the roses—the technique for the lifelike leaves is on page 24.

2. Mold the box. Use this quick professional method for a box with strong, evenly thick walls. Melt two pounds of coating and fill bottom of Heart mold box to the brim. Place on floor of freezer for about four minutes to harden the shell. Empty the liquid coating and replace in freezer for about four minutes until shell is hardened and pulls away from mold. Unmold.

For the lid, use coating remaining from bottom of box. Use the color contrast method described on page 34. First fill the beaded areas of mold with melted white coating and tube 2. Let this set up, then fill the ruffled area with melted pink coating and tube 2, let set up, then fill the entire lid mold with chocolate-flavored coating. Harden in freezer about ten minutes.

3. Pipe name on lid with tube 1 and a mixture of half royal icing, half piping gel. Attach made-ahead roses with dots of melted coating. Trim off bases of roses as necessary. Add leaves.

Holiday brandied cherries

America's favorite! This candy rated four stars from a panel of tasters.

   16-ounce jar maraschino
      cherries without stems
   1 cup brandy (approximate)
   1 pound dry fondant
      (approximate)
   1½ pounds dark chocolate,
      tempered for dipping

Days before you begin, thoroughly drain the juice from the cherries. Place drained cherries in a jar and fill it with brandy. Cover the jar. Allow cherries to soak for at least two days—a week is even better.

1. Drain the brandy-soaked cherries thoroughly. Place about ten cherries in a bowl with a rounded bottom. Rotate the bowl rapidly so the cherries roll briskly around the sides. Toss a spoonful of the dry fondant into the bowl as you continue rotating it. As soon as the cherries have picked up all the fondant, add a little more. When the cherries appear dry, add a spoonful of the reserved brandy, then more fondant. Never stop rotating the bowl. Repeat the process three or four times until the cherries have built up a coating of brandy and fondant and resemble round pink balls. Coat the remaining cherries.

2. As soon as all the cherries are coated, dip them in tempered chocolate (at right). If you delay, the coating will break down. Make sure they are well coated with chocolate. If you see a spot not covered on a candy, touch it up with a little chocolate. Candies will "leak" unless the center has an air-tight chocolate coating. Store in a cool place for a day or two before serving. The fondant will have changed into a delightful cordial, with a flavorsome cherry swimming inside the chocolate shell. Store in a covered box in a cool place for up to three weeks. Yield: about 70 candies.

Note: Brandied cherries are best made by a congenial group. As one person tempers the chocolate, a second rotates the bowl and a third adds fondant and brandy.

For these luxurious candies, you'll want to dip in *real chocolate*. It's an easy job to temper chocolate, if you keep a low-temperature thermometer at hand.

How to temper chocolate*

1. Chop about 1½ pounds of either milk or dark chocolate.

2. Fill lower pan of a one-quart double boiler with hot water at about 140°F. Use your thermometer to check temperature. Put about one-fourth of the chopped chocolate in top pan of double boiler and set in position on lower pan. Stir the chocolate vigorously as it melts, scraping the sides and bottom of the pan with rubber scraper. When the chocolate in the pan is almost melted, add a second fourth of chopped chocolate. Stir vigorously, just as before, until the chocolate is nearly melted. Continue adding chocolate, stirring as it melts until all the chocolate is melted.

At all times, make very sure no water gets into chocolate. Even a small amount of water will make chocolate stiffen.

3. Replace the hot water in the lower pan of the double boiler with cold water. Now stir the chocolate vigorously until the temperature of the chocolate is cooled to 83°F.

4. Replace the cold water in the lower pan with water at 85°F. Check with thermometer. Leave the upper pan over the lower pan to hold the chocolate at dipping temperature. Now the chocolate is ready for dipping. Test by dipping the tip of a knife blade into the chocolate. Place knife in refrigerator for just one minute. Chocolate will set up and look glossy.

Please turn the page

Dipping the cherry centers*

Set coated cherries on a cookie sheet to left of pan of tempered chocolate. Place a cookie sheet covered with waxed paper and lightly dusted with flour on the right side. With your left hand, drop a center into the chocolate. With your right hand, tumble with a dipping fork to completely cover, then lift it out with the fork under it. Tap the stem of the fork sharply on the side of the pan so excess chocolate will drop off. Move your hand to the prepared cookie sheet and give a quick turn of your wrist so the dipped center will drop off, upside down. Once the center has been deposited on the cookie sheet, do not move it. This would thin the chocolate covering. Stir the chocolate with the fork from time to time to keep all of it at a uniform temperature.

After you've completed dipping the cherries, slide the cookie sheet into the refrigerator for five minutes only. This will give a final "snap" to the chocolate. Complete hardening at room temperature. Place candies in paper candy cups, then in a closed box.

Is marshmallow her favorite center? Try this lucious version.

    2 tablespoons unflavored gelatin
    ½ cup cold water
    2 cups granulated sugar
    ¾ cup light corn syrup
    ¾ cup hot water
    1 teaspoon flavoring
    ½ cup finely chopped candied
        cherries or candied pineapple
    few drops of food color

Before you begin, line the bottom of a 10″ square pan with porous paper.

1. Combine gelatin and ½ cup cold water in large mixer bowl. Meanwhile, combine sugar, corn syrup and ¾ cup hot water in a three-quart heavy saucepan. Place over high heat and stir constantly with a wooden spoon until all sugar crystals are dissolved. Wash down sides of pan with a pastry brush dipped in hot water, then clip on thermometer. Cook without stirring to 245°F. Wash down sides of pan twice more while mixture cooks. Remove pan from heat.

2. Set mixer at highest speed. As you beat, slowly pour hot syrup in a thin stream over gelatin in bowl. Continue beating for about 15 minutes, or until ribbons dropped off the beater retain their shape on the surface. Add flavoring and color toward end of beating. Fold in fruit. Pour into prepared pan, smoothing with a spatula dipped in cold water. Firm overnight at room temperature.

4. To unmold, loosen edges with a knife. Turn out onto pan containing a mixture of ¼ cup confectioners' sugar, ¼ cup cornstarch. Lay a folded moist towel on paper, then peel off damp paper. Cut into 1″ strips with a scissors dipped in cold water. Tumble strips, cut into 1″ squares, tumble again.

5. Dip the marshmallows in tempered chocolate, as described at left. First brush off excess cornstarch mixture. Yield: 100 chocolate marshmallows, or about 25 eggs.

*From *The Complete Wilton Book of Candy*

easy to do! Decorate a rosy Mini-tier cake, very simply. Trim it with fabric flowers, then set it in a ring of flowers. A Valentine vision!

1. Bake three single layers in Mini-tier pans. Ice tiers. Assemble two 9″ heart separator plates with 5″ clear pillars. Set bottom tier on it. Place other two tiers on mini-tier plates.

2. Simple but elegant borders form the trim. Pipe tube 103 sweet pea borders at base of all tiers. Pipe a petal against side of tier, then one on plate. Continue around tier. At top of each tier pipe a tube 16 shell border. Just within it, pipe a tube 103 curve, jiggle your hand twice, then pipe another curve. Use a continuous motion to complete this "rhythm" border. Finish with tube 101s bows on tier sides.

3. Set Flower holder ring on bottom 9″ plate with pillars. Wedge small blocks of styrofoam into ring, then arrange fabric flowers. Add a few tulle poufs for an airy effect. Place a small circle of clear plastic wrap in centers of all three tiers. Arrange a few fabric flowers on two lower tier tops. Set bottom tier on 5″ pillars. Assemble with two upper tiers and mini-tier legs.

For top ornament, wire a few flowers to stick of a pink lollipop. Insert stick into top tier. Serve this *Quick & Pretty* Valentine to twelve.

 **is for <u>Wonderful</u> <u>Wedding</u> cakes**

Here we present a little bouquet of bridal cakes, each charming, each sure to make the decorator and the bride very proud and happy.

Cloud nine

The airy trims on this cake are piped on Australian nails. They give a very lacy, dimensional effect, but are no harder to do than lattice.

Accessories you'll need:
Australian nails—crescent, border, basket and arch shapes
Bride and groom figures
Plate from Heart ornament base
Six 7″ Corinthian pillars
Four 5″ Corinthian pillars
Two 13″ and two 9″ separator plates

1. Pipe lace pieces. You will need 18 crescents, 14 borders, seven baskets and eight curves piped on the arch nail. Be sure to make extras. Grease the nails well with solid white vegetable shortening. Use Egg white royal icing to pipe tube 1 lattice directly on the nail. Be sure to keep all piping ⅛″ away from open sides of nail. Trim edges with dots, then stick nail in styrofoam to dry. For arch design on top tier, tape *Celebrate!* pattern to nail, tape wax paper over it, grease the nail, then pipe. To remove lace from nail, place in open oven set at lowest heat for a minute to melt the shortening. Gently slide lace piece off nail.

2. Pipe many royal icing drop flowers with tubes 23, 35, 225 and 129. Add tube 2 centers. Attach about one third of the flowers to fine wire stems. Make tulle poufs by bunching centers of 3″ squares of tulle with wire. Twist stems of 18 flowers and four poufs together. Form a circle with the twisted stems to form a base for the bouquet. You'll need seven bouquets. Attach flowers to edge of plate with icing. Ice bride and groom figures to plate.

3. Prepare lower separator plates. Clip off two opposite pillar projections on plates and replace each by gluing on two stud plates. The plates will now have six evenly spaced projections.

4. Prepare the two-layer tiers—16″, 12″ and 8″ round. The 8″ tier should be 3″ high, other tiers 4″ high. Bake, fill and ice, then assemble on separator plates with pillars. Divide base tier into sixths, corresponding to pillars. Mark at top edge. Make a second series of marks ½″ above base of tier, half way between marks at top. Divide middle tier into eighths, using pillars as guide, and mark at top edge. Divide side of tier into sixteenths and mark 1½″ up from base. Divide top tier into eighths and mark midway on side. Mark center backs of all tiers. Take tiers apart to decorate.

5. On base tier, pipe a tube 8 bottom ball border and drape with tube 2 string. Edge separator plate with tube 5. With pillars in position, pipe a line of royal icing around bottom of a basket and set on plate between pillars. Pipe a line of icing around circular base of bouquet and gently place in basket. Repeat for six baskets.

6. On middle tier, pipe a tube 7 ball border at base. Drop double tube 2 string from mark to mark and top points with dots. With pillars in position, attach a basket and bouquet to center of separator plate, just as for base tier. Edge plate with tube 5.

7. On top tier, pipe a tube 5 bottom ball border. Drop triple tube 2 strings from mark to mark and top points with dots.

8. Reassemble tiers and add final trims. It's easiest to do this when the cake is on the reception table. *Be sure to work from the top down.* On top tier, attach plate, with couple, to center of tier. Pipe a line of icing on bottom of an arch lace piece and set on edge of tier between marks. Continue to surround tier. Attach flowers in tiny cascades between lace pieces. On middle tier, attach lace borders on mounds of icing at each mark. Complete top border with tube 5 balls. Attach flowers in cascades. On bottom tier, attach lace borders on mounds of icing at marks. Complete border with tube 7 balls. Attach a crescent lace piece to center of cake side at mark. Pipe a line of icing around edges of piece and hold gently to cake. Attach a crescent lace piece on either side of first. Continue around cake. Mound flowers around sides of borders and add little clusters at points of crescents. Cloud Nine is a dream cake! Serve two lower tiers to 186 guests.

Cloud Nine

147

Wonderful Wedding Cakes

Rose perfume

Fresh flowers, easily arranged in a flower ring, add beauty and fragrance to this lovely cake. You will need two Flower spikes, six 7" Corinthian pillars, two 8" round plates, six stud plates, Kissing lovebirds and a Flower ring.

1. Clip off pillar projections on plates and glue on six evenly spaced stud plates. Prepare tiers—a 14" two layer and an 8" two-layer round, plus a 6" single layer. Fill, ice and assemble with pillars and plates. Divide 14" tier into fourteenths and mark at top edge. Divide 8" tier into tenths and mark 1" above base. Decorate assembled cake.

2. On base tier, run a tube 10 line of icing around bottom. Cover with a tube 70 shell-motion border. Pipe tube 18 double zig-zag garlands at top edge from mark to mark. Add tube 352 leaves between each. Using garlands as guides, pipe a tube 13 curving vine on tier side. Trim with tube 352 leaves.

3. On 8" tier, pipe tube 16 zig-zag garlands from mark to mark, letting them drape below plate. Add tube 352 leaves. Do top border with tube 16 shells.

4. On top tier, pipe a tube 67 shell-motion border at bottom. Using 8" tier as guide, pull out tube 13 curving stems from top edge. Add trios of tube 67 leaves. Do top shell border with tube 16.

5. Fill Flower ring with blocks of oasis, moisten and arrange flowers in ring. When cake is on the reception table, carefully lift top tiers off pillars, set ring in position and replace tiers. Set lovebirds on cake top, then push in Flower spikes behind them. Fill with water with an eye dropper and arrange more flowers. Serve two lower tiers of Rose Perfume to 122 guests.

Everything's coming up roses

Every tier is graced with delicate pink and apricot roses! You will need two 7" and two 11" round separator plates, four 5" and four 7" Corinthian pillars, Cupid in bird bath figure, Bridal couple and the plate from Heart ornament.

1. Pipe royal icing roses with tubes 101 and 103. Also pipe tiny rosebuds with tube 101s.

2. Prepare tiers. You will need a single-layer 16" round and two-layer 14" x 4", 10" x 4" and 6" x 3" tiers. Fill, ice and assemble with plates and pillars. Divide 16" tier into 24ths and mark at top edge. Divide 14" tier into fourths, corresponding to pillars, and mark at top edge. Divide each of these spaces into thirds and mark 1½" below top. Divide 10" tier into twelfths and mark midway on side. Divide top tier into tenths and mark at base.

3. On 16" tier, pipe a tube 20 star border at base. Drop double tube 2 strings from marks at top. Do top shell border with tube 17. On 14" tier, pipe bottom shell border with tube 20. Drop string guidelines from marks and pipe tube 17 zig-zag garlands. Drape with tube 2 strings. Pipe a tube 20 reverse shell top border. Edge separator plate wih tube 13 and an "e" motion.

4. On 10" tier, pipe a tube 17 shell border at base. Drop string guidelines and pipe tube 17 garlands from mark to mark. Drape with tube 2 string, then top with tube 14 fleurs-de-lis and stars. Do top shell border with tube 17, edge separator plate with tube 13.

5. On top tier, pipe puff garlands with tube 17 and trim with tube 2 string. Do top shell border with tube 17. Now mound icing on cake top and press in roses. Add a ribbon bow on a toothpick. Set cupid within pillars and trim with rosebuds. Circle the 10" tier with

Please turn the page

Sunshine

The simplicity of this sweet cake is set off by sprays and garlands of golden flowers. Make the flowers ahead of time, then decorating the cake will go quickly.

Accessories you'll need:
   Two 13" Hexagon
      separator plates
   Six 7" Corinthian pillars
   Bride and groom figures
   Plate from Heart ornament base
   Kissing lovebirds for top tier

1. In advance, pipe royal icing flowers. Do roses with tubes 102 and 103, sweet peas with tube 104. Dry. Attach bridal couple to plate with icing.

2. Prepare the two-layer tiers. Base tier is 16" round, middle tier is a 12" hexagon. Top tier is 8" round. Two lower tiers are 4" high, top tier is 3" high. Assemble with pillars and plates.

Using pillars as guide, mark side of base tier 1" below top for six flower garlands. Divide remaining six spaces in two. Divide top tier into sixteenths and mark 1" up from base. Mark center back of all tiers and take apart to decorate.

3. On base tier, pipe a tube 504 bottom shell border. Drop string guidelines for large and small garlands. Pipe garlands with tube 502 zigzags. Pipe scallops on tier top with tube 15, then do top shell border with tube 502. Edge separator plate with tube 15.

4. On middle tier, pipe bottom shell border with tube 501. Use same tube to pull up triple upright shells at corners. Add fleurs-de-lis and stars. Do top shell border with tube 501.

5. On top tier, use tube 501 to pipe bottom shell border and top reverse shell border. Drop tube 14 strings from mark to mark. Add

rosettes at points with same tube.

6. Attach love birds on cake top with icing. Secure plate, with couple, within pillars. Starting at top of cake, trim with flowers. Mound icing around lovebirds and arrange several roses and sprays of sweet peas. Make cascades on middle tier, each with one rose surrounded with sweet peas. Add tiny ribbon bows on toothpicks. Make a curve of roses and sweet peas around bridal couple. Attach roses and sweet peas to large garlands on base tier. Trim all roses with tube 66 leaves. Your sunny cake is beautiful! Serve two lower tiers to 168 guests.

Everything's roses
shown on page 149

roses on mounds of icing. Attach couple to plate and set within pillars. Trim plate with tiny rosebuds. Form cascades of roses on 14" tier and accent garlands with more roses. Trim all flowers with tube 65 leaves. Serve three lower tiers of this rosy vision to 198 guests.

A simply delicious chocolate groom's cake

1. Make a recipe of luxurious Chocolate ganache (page 86) and pipe 16 roses with tube 102. Put in freezer while you prepare the cake.

2. Bake two layers of his favorite chocolate cake in 9" x 13" pans. Fill and ice with the ganache, set on cake board.

3. Pipe message in buttercream with tube 1. Edge base of cake with tube 1D. Pipe a tube 15 shell bottom border and tube 2 beading at top of tube 1D strip. On top of cake, pipe a wide border with tube 789. Pipe a tube 15 outer shell border, a tube 2 inner bead border. Position roses evenly on top of cake and at each corner of base. Finish with trios of tube 67 leaves. Serve your trimly tailored confection to 54 wedding guests.

Serving and cutting charts for wedding, groom's and party cakes

To cut wedding (or groom's) cakes, start at the top. Remove top tier and box. Remove next tier down, slice and serve. Continue working your way down the tiers. Bottom tier is cut last.

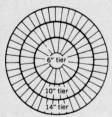

For a round tier move in 2" from the outer edge, cut a circle and cut 1" wide slices within it. Move in another two inches, cut another circle, and slice into 1" pieces. Continue until entire tier is cut.

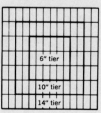

For a square tier move in 2" from outer edge and cut straight across. Slice into 1" pieces. Move in another 2" and slice this section into 1" pieces. Continue until entire tier is cut.

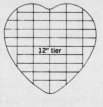

Divide heart tiers in 2" vertical rows. Slice 1" pieces from each row.

Petal and hexagon tiers are cut like round tiers.

Wedding and groom's cakes

Servings are 1" wide by 2" deep, two layers high. Top tier is usually frozen for the first anniversary.

SHAPE	SIZE	SERVINGS
ROUND	6"	16
	8"	30
	10"	48
	12"	68
	14"	92
	16"	118
	18"	148
SQUARE	6"	18
	8"	32
	10"	50
	12"	72
	14"	98
	16"	128
	18"	162
HEXAGON	6"	6
	9"	22
	12"	50
	15"	66
PETAL	6"	8
	9"	20
	12"	44
	15"	62
HEART	6"	12
	9"	28
	12"	48
	15"	90

Shower and party cakes

Servings are ample dessert-sized portions, each two-layer. Most one-mix cakes serve twelve.

SHAPE	SIZE	SERVINGS
ROUND	6"	6
	8"	10
	10"	14
	12"	22
	14"	36
SQUARE	6"	8
	8"	12
	10"	20
	12"	36
	14"	42
RECTANGLE	9" x 13"	24
	11" x 15"	35
	12" x 18"	54
HEART	6"	6
	9"	12
	12"	24
HEXAGON	6"	6
	9"	12
	12"	20
PETAL	6"	6
	9"	8
	12"	26
OVAL	7" x 9"	12

 is for e<u>X</u>pert advice from our decorating staff—ways to make work easier, cakes prettier

To guide script or letters, stretch a thread across the iced cake top to mark a line so lightly it will never be seen on the completed cake.

For quick release of lace pieces, lily nail piped flowers or Color Flow, use non-stick pan release. Spray it on the foil lining of your lily nail, and give a quick whoosh to the wax paper covering your patterns.

Use cookie cutters as pattern presses. You'll be amazed at the attractive patterns you can create in a hurry. Sets of round, star and heart cutters are very handy. Gum paste flower cutters work well, too.

Transfer patterns quickly the piping gel way. Trace pattern on parchment or wax paper. Place tracing upside down and outline main lines with tube 1 and gel. When icing on cake top crusts, lay paper on cake, gel side next to cake. Press lightly with fingers to make sure gel adheres to cake. Remove paper and pipe inner outlines right on gel. On outer edges of design, pipe outlines just outside of gel lines. Fill-in icing holds firmly. Pipe details freehand.

Cake icer tube 789 makes fast work of icing sides of cakes. Just run the tube around the bottom, then the upper area of the cake side, overlapping as needed. Smooth with a spatula.

A pipe cutter is a handy and inexpensive little tool when constructing a tier cake with dowels. Insert dowel, lift up and clip, then push down .

A hot spatula, not a wet one, smooths buttercream icing. Dip knife in hot water to heat it, wipe off and smooth your icing. Your cake will be as smooth as any shown in this book.

Leveling a cake is easy and accurate with a thread. Let cake stand five minutes in pan after removing from oven. Draw a taut thread across it with a sawing motion, pressing ends of thread on edges of pan. Remove scraps. A perfect 2" thick layer!

Store extra icing compactly. Scrape out onto a length of clear plastic, then wrap just as you would a package. Stack in the refrigerator. Takes much less room than containers—and you can identify colors at a glance.

Please a bride and groom! When making a wedding cake, bake a 9" single-layer heart cake, too. Decorate it in the style of the wedding cake. Box the heart cake, adding two paper plates, napkins and plastic forks. This is the honeymooners' own treat. (They're usually too nervous to even taste the cake at the reception!)

Save all flowers left over from a decorating project. They'll be life-savers when you need to trim a cake in a hurry. Royal icing flowers boxed in clear plastic keep almost indefinitely on your cupboard shelf.

A pound of confectionery coating, melted, yields about two cups. Good to remember when you are molding a hollow shell such as the heart box on page 142. Fill the mold with water, then measure, to determine how much coating you will need.

Popcorn lovers! ⅔ cup of kernels will make four to six quarts of popped corn, depending on brand.

Cut a cake board the exact shape of any irregularly-shaped cake by using a compass. Place the pan the cake was baked in upside down on corrugated cardboard. Adjust the compass so points are one or two inches apart—or the margin you would like around your cake.

Hold the compass with needle point against pan, point with lead extending out on cardboard. Move the compass around the pan. The lead will draw an outline exactly the shape of your cake, but larger.

To seal in filling between layers and give a smooth side to your cake, pipe a line of icing around edge of base layer. Use any large tube. Spread filling on layer within icing line, then add upper layer.

Flowers look prettier on a cake top when some of them are given a lift. To do this, ice a marshmallow to the cake top, then set the flower on it. Use a large or small marshmallow, according to the size of your flower. Conceal with leaves or other flowers.

Script pipes smoothly when you thin the icing with piping gel.

Smooth the icing on a rounded area by brushing with a damp artist's brush. Dip the brush in water, then shake before using.

Always chill your cakes before icing them. Layers are firmer and easier to handle. If you need to "carve" a shape, a chilled cake cuts more smoothly.

 is for cakes for the <u>Youngest</u> family members . . . flowered, flounced and sweet as Baby

The sweetest, daintiest, prettiest cake you could create for a baby shower or christening party! Use your egg pan to shape the bassinet, a People mold figure for the baby.

Mold the baby

1. Make a recipe of rolled fondant, tint a small amount a delicate flesh color and mold in the 5-year-old child mold. Mold head and upper body only, pressing firmly into the mold and following directions in the booklet that comes with the mold. Smooth seams with a damp finger. Model a "log" of rolled fondant the diameter of the baby's waistline and about 1" long. Attach to waistline and dry.

2. Make up the face as directed in the booklet. Pipe tiny tight curls with tube 1s and royal icing.

Make the bassinet

1. Pipe lace pieces with egg white royal icing and *Celebrate!* pattern.

2. Pipe the hood of the bassinet on the egg pan. Turn pan rounded side up and lightly grease with solid white shortening. Mark a line to divide pan in half. The wider curve of the pan will shape the hood. Do all piping with egg white royal icing and tube 2. Pipe over the marked line for front of hood. Pipe a perpendicular line from center of front, curving to center of base of pan. Pipe radiating lines on either side of this to form the shape. Overpipe front edge and base for strength. Connect radiating lines with scallops. Dry thoroughly. To remove hood, place pan in warm oven for just a moment or two to melt shortening. Gently slide hood off pan.

3. Bake a firm pound cake in an egg half-pan. Chill and flatten at base. Place flat side down on work surface. Ice rounded side with buttercream, then cover with rolled fondant. Turn over, ice, then cover top with fondant.

4. Model a little pillow from rolled fondant, about 3½" wide x 2". Place on bassinet, at wide end of egg, then cover with a rectangle of fondant for pillow case. Indent in center for baby's head. Using pan as pattern, cut out fondant blanket, measuring 7" from narrower curve of pan. Place baby figure in bassinet and drape blanket over it. Trim blanket and pillow case with tube 1s dot flowers and scallops. Tint fondant pale pink, roll out and cut plaque, using pan as pattern. Dry flat.

Make the cake

1. Pipe lots of drop flowers with tubes 225, 131 and 139 with royal icing and varied shades of pink.

2. Bake, fill and ice a two-layer 9" x 13" cake. Set on serving tray.

Divide short sides of cake into fifths, long sides into sevenths, and mark midway on sides. Press a small heart cutter in centers of long sides. Outline with tube 2 bulbs and write name with tube 1s.

3. Pipe bottom and top shell borders with tube 16. Drape tube 126 swags from mark to mark. Set plaque on cake top and frame with flowers. Mound icing at corners of cake and attach flowers in cascades. Top swags with flowers. Trim flowers with tube 65 leaves.

4. Attach bassinet to plaque with icing. Secure flowers to bassinet. Now pipe a tube 2 line of icing around larger curve of bassinet and set hood in position. Border bassinet and hood with tube 2 beading. Attach lace pieces by piping a dot of icing on base, then holding to bead borders. Wire a ribbon bow to a toothpick and press in to center back of bassinet. Your christening cake is complete—and just darling! Serve cake to 24 guests.

Quick & very Pretty sheet cakes for

It won't take long to decorate a sweet centerpiece cake that will be the talk of the shower party. Both are easy-to-serve sheet cakes, decorated with only basic techniques.

Quick & Pretty

I'd like a boy, but a girl would be great!

Two cute baby faces set the theme for the party. A surprise! They're made from rolled fondant and shaped with cookie cutters.

1. Make a half-recipe of rolled fondant and tint one-third flesh color, one-third blue and one-third pink. Cut out two hearts with 3½″

cutters from flesh-colored fondant for faces. Cut pink and blue bonnets with the same cutter, then trim off in a curve. Cut out pink cheeks with a 1″ round Miniature cutter. Use a 1½″ cutter for the small heart and a Truffle cutter for the flowers. Assemble the faces with dots of buttercream and let all pieces dry flat.

2. Bake, fill and ice a two-layer 9″ x 13″ cake. Starting 1½″ in from each corner, divide long sides of cake in thirds. Divide short sides of cake in halves, starting 1½″ in from corners.

3. Pipe tube 16 shell borders on

bottom and top of cake. Drop string guidelines for curves from mark to mark, then pipe tube 124 ruffles on sides. Edge with tube 3 bulbs. Pipe message on cake top with tube 2, inserting small pink heart. Pipe a tube 124 ruffle around top edge of cake and edge with tube 3 bulbs.

4. Place heart faces on cake top. Pipe lips and eyes with tube 4. Do hair-do's with tube 2. On boy's bonnet, pipe a tube 5 zig-zag edging and a tube 2 pompon. Pipe a tube 101 double ruffle on girl's bonnet. Finish bonnet trim with tube 101 bows. Now add the posy trims, attaching with dots of icing.

Serve to 24 party guests.

Quick and Pretty
A carriage for baby
This cute little carriage is quickly piped with an easy pattern you do yourself.

1. Pipe royal icing drop flowers with tubes 35 and 225. Add tube 2 centers and dry.

2. Bake, fill and ice a two-layer 9" x 13" cake. Divide long sides of cake into tenths, short sides into eighths and mark 1" above base. For shape of carriage, lightly press a 9" x 7" oval pan on cake top. Use a 3½" round cutter to define wheels. Divide circles into fourths, then eighths and mark for spokes. Mark a pie-shaped wedge on oval for opening of carriage. On hood, press a 2" heart cutter.

3. Write message on cake top with tube 1, then outline carriage with tube 3. Outline wheels with tube 5. Fill in carriage with tube 14 stars, starting with pink heart. Over-pipe wheels and spokes with tube 5.

4. Pipe tube 16 shell borders at bottom and top of cake. Drop strings from mark to mark with tube 16. Now trim carriage and cake sides with flowers, attaching with dots of icing. Serve to 24 shower guests.

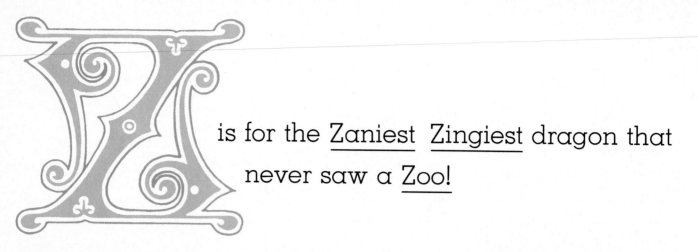

Z is for the Zaniest Zingiest dragon that never saw a Zoo!

Isn't he loveable? Make him for a child's birthday, a just-for-fun centerpiece, or just to show what cake and icing can create! Our zany dragon is delicious, too. He's entirely edible from his egg minicake head through his bowling pin pan body to his marshmallow tail.

1. The pointed scales that grow down his back are made of Candy Melt™ confectionery coating. Melt and tint the coating and spread it about ⅛" thick on a piece of foil, taped to the back of a cookie sheet, shiny side up. Let the coating just set up, but not completely harden, at room temperature. With a ruler and a sharp artist's knife cut into triangles about 1" wide at base. Cut some smaller triangles for tapering tail. Harden completely in the refrigerator, then run a spatula under the foil to release triangles. Save scraps to melt again.

2. This gentle creature clutches a bouquet. Pipe the flowers in royal icing with tube 191. Add tube 3 centers and dry.

3. Build the figure from a firm pound cake recipe. You will need a cake baked in the Bowling pin pan for his body, two Egg minicakes for the head and two more for his feet. Fill the two

halves of the bowling pin cake, chill, then trim off the top of the bowling pin. Start about 3" from top and slant down. Ice these two half-pieces to the lower sides of the bowling pin as upper legs. Ice two egg minicakes together, chill and attach to top of bowling pin with toothpicks for head. Set figure on serving tray and position remaining egg cakes for feet.

4. Now for the dragon's tail. Thread three large marshmallows on a 9" length of florists' wire. Add four miniature marshmallows. Insert end of wire into back of dragon and curve for tail.

5. Bring the dragon to life. Figure pipe arms with tube 2A, starting with light pressure, and increasing pressure, as you move down. Mark a long oval on front of dragon and mark his mouth on head. Pipe ears with tube 5, drawing to a point. Now fill in with tube 18 stars, using a lighter tint of icing to fill in oval. Pipe whites of eyes with a tube 5 ball and center with flattened tube 3 dots. Pipe smile with tube 3 and do the nostrils with the same tube, using a spiral motion. Pipe fangs and nails with tube 5. Attach flowers, then pipe tube 2 stems. Finish off your zany dragon by pressing the candy triangles into his back and tail. Serve this friendly pet to twelve.

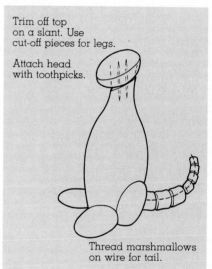

Trim off top on a slant. Use cut-off pieces for legs.

Attach head with toothpicks.

Thread marshmallows on wire for tail.

Index